Horatio N. Warren

Two Reunions of the 142d Regiment, Pa. Vols.

Including a history of the regiment, a description of the Battle of Gettysburg, also a complete roster of the regiment

Horatio N. Warren

Two Reunions of the 142d Regiment, Pa. Vols.
Including a history of the regiment, a description of the Battle of Gettysburg, also a complete roster of the regiment

ISBN/EAN: 9783337402587

Printed in Europe, USA, Canada, Australia, Japan

Cover: Foto ©ninafisch / pixelio.de

More available books at **www.hansebooks.com**

TWO REUNIONS

OF THE

142d Regiment, Pa. Vols.

INCLUDING

A HISTORY OF THE REGIMENT, DEDICATION OF
THE MONUMENT, A DESCRIPTION OF
THE BATTLE OF GETTYSBURG,

ALSO

A COMPLETE ROSTER OF THE REGIMENT.

BY COL. HORATIO N. WARREN.

PREFACE.

THE object to be attained in the publication of this book, as decided by the surviving members of the One Hundred and Forty-second Pennsylvania Volunteers, at their reunion at Gettysburg, Pa., September 11, 1889, was to have in the family of each member of the regiment, who would subscribe for the same, a complete roster of the regiment, with a short history of its honorable service, including an account of our two reunions, believing that such a book will be treasured by our children, families and friends, when we shall have joined that great army of our comrades, who gave their lives for the Union and in suppressing the most gigantic rebellion recorded in history. The records of the War Department show that there were only two regiments in the service of the Union army whose percentage of losses sustained by reason of their participation in the battles for the Union will exceed those of the One Hundred and Forty-second Pennsylvania Volunteers. Nine hundred and thirty-five men and officers were enlisted. Eight hundred and eleven of them were killed, wounded and taken prisoners during their term of service, which commenced in August, 1862, and ended when peace was declared in the year 1865.

CONTENTS.

	PAGE.
FIRST REUNION,	7
ADDRESS OF COL. H. N. WARREN,	7
SURVIVORS OF THE ONE HUNDRED AND FORTY-SECOND REGIMENT,	10
SECOND REUNION,	13
HISTORY OF THE REGIMENT, BY COL. H. N. WARREN,	14
DEDICATION OF MONUMENT,	45
ADDRESS OF COL. H. N. WARREN,	47
ADDRESS OF CAPT. GEORGE R. SNOWDEN,	48
ADDRESS OF PRIVATE JAMES E. MACLANE,	54
ADDRESS OF LIEUT. JOHN V. MILLER,	58
ADDRESS OF PRIVATE D. J. HORNER,	60
INSCRIPTION ON MONUMENT,	61
ROSTER OF THE ONE HUNDRED AND FORTY-SECOND REGIMENT, PA. VOLS.,	63
APPENDIX,	85
DESCRIPTION OF THE BATTLE OF GETTYSBURG,	87
THE VALLEY OF THE SHADOW OF DEATH,	116
JOHN BURNS OF GETTYSBURG,	118
BATTLE HYMN OF THE REPUBLIC,	121
RED, WHITE AND BLUE,	122
BARBARA FRIETCHIE,	123
MARCHING THROUGH GEORGIA,	125
SHERIDAN'S RIDE,	126
SCOTT AND THE VETERAN,	128
TENTING ON THE OLD CAMP-GROUND,	129
THE STAR-SPANGLED BANNER,	130
THE SWORD OF BUNKER HILL,	131
THE BATTLE-CRY OF FREEDOM,	132
THE COMMON CHORD,	133
A WARRIOR BOLD,	134

CONTENTS.

APPENDIX:

	PAGE.
"Yes, I'm Guilty,"	135
Our Two Opinions,	137
America,	138
Ode for Decoration Day,	139
Speed Away,	141
Old Oaken Bucket,	142
Annie Laurie,	143
Banty Tim,	143
Louisiana Lowlands,	145
Kingdom Coming,	146
Old Folks at Home,	147
What are the Wild Waves Saying?	148
Home, Sweet Home,	148
The Jiners,	149
Auld Lang Syne,	152

FIRST REUNION

HELD AT

GETTYSBURG, JULY 1, 1888.

IN accordance with previous notice, a Reunion of the Survivors of the 142d Regiment of Pennsylvania Volunteers was held at 11 o'clock A. M., in the historic grove adjoining the Seminary building. A remnant of about thirty veterans of the regiment assembled, and was joined by several members of the 121st Regiment, which fought by the side of the 142d on that memorable 1st of July, 1863.

On motion of Captain George R. Snowden, of Company I (now Brigadier-General in command of the 1st Brigade National Guard of Pennsylvania), Colonel Horatio N. Warren, who was promoted to the command of the regiment after the resignation of Lieutenant-Colonel McCalmont, was made Chairman of the meeting, and First Sergeant John J. Hoffman, of Company C, was chosen Secretary.

On taking the chair, Colonel Warren delivered an eloquent and touching address, which was warmly received and frequently applauded.

ADDRESS OF COL. H. N. WARREN.

COMRADES: It is with many pleasurable emotions and a grateful heart to the Ruler of the Universe, that I am permitted, after the lapse of a quarter of a century, and under the present auspices, to look once again into the honest and brave faces of men whose associations with me during three years of a bloody and cruel war, make me realize and fully understand, beyond the peradventure of a doubt, that all of them are my friends, are the friends of my country, strong and true, having been over a score of times under a hot fire, and never found wanting.

The trials and tribulations through which we passed during those three long years from 1862 to 1865, in my mind were calculated to build up in our hearts a kindly feeling for each other that time can never efface, and death alone destroy.

Our meeting here to-day, my comrades, possibly more than to any like number of men among the many thousands who will congregate upon this wide, world-renowned battle-field, is of great significance, because to us it has a two-fold meaning.

This is the anniversary of Gettysburg, where was fought the greatest battle that was ever waged in the western hemisphere, if not in the world, and in which from its inception the old 142d Pennsylvania Volunteers, of which we are the living representatives, took an active and honorable part, as her long list of killed and wounded and our terribly depleted ranks told, after the smoke of battle had cleared away, and we halted for a few hours to sorrowfully bury our dead, care for our wounded, and sum up the results of the terrible carnage made necessary for our victory.

We are not here to-day to exult over that victory, for we realize that the quarter of a century that has sped away on the wings of time since then, has to a great extent wiped out the bitter feeling we then entertained towards our southern brothers; and we believe to-day that a large proportion of those men still living, who were against us then, are now lovers of the old Union, and are favorably inclined to rejoice with us that at Gettysburg, Pa., the tide of Lee's invasion was checked, the backbone of the rebellion broken, and that it was also here that Secession lost her grip; and here, upon this sacred soil, made memorable because of the sacrifice of so many precious lives, I hesitate not to believe that now, with us, they would be willing to register a vow that the old Union, organized and established by our forefathers, north and south, has been made stronger and more enduring by reason of the sacrifice it took to perpetuate its existence.

This is our first reunion. We are here, comrades, to renew our friendships, and to form a fraternal society among those of us who live, that will be instrumental in bringing us together occasionally, and in renewing the old love that was born while we marched shoulder to shoulder, perpetuate a loving memory of the comrades who gave up their lives on our country's altar, and of those of our number who have since those days passed over the river to their long homes, towards which we are all speeding so rapidly. If we accomplish this, I am sure it will be a great source of pleasure to us in our declining years, and teach our children loyalty to the flag which is so precious to each one of us, that whenever our eyes rest upon its beautiful folds, an inexpressible feeling comes over us, causing our blood to course through our veins more rapidly—at least, comrades, this is so with me.

I am too thoroughly delighted by reason of our meeting to-day, to continue to any length. The old 142d Pennsylvania Volunteers has a record which none of us need be ashamed of. Enlisted in June and July, 1862, it was organized as a regiment in August following, sent to the front immediately after its organization, remained there in active service until General Lee at Appomattox surrendered to General Grant, which virtually ended the war. As my memory serves me, I will name the battles in which we participated, in their regular order:

1. Fredericksburgh, Va., Dec. 3, 1862.
2. Burnside Mud March.
3. Chancellorsville.
4. Gettysburg, Pa.
5. Frankstown, Md.
6. Thoroughfare Gap, Va.
7. Rappahannock Station.
8. Meade's Retrograde Movement.
9. Wilderness.
10. Laurel Hill.
11. Spottsylvania.
12. Tolopotomy Creek.
13. North Anna River.
14. Cold Harbor.
15. Petersburgh, 18th of June, and under fire every day for three months.
16. Weldon Railroad.
17. Hatcher's Run.
18. Chapin Farm.
19. Hatcher's Run.
20. Dabney's Mill.
21. Weldon Railroad Raid.
22. Fort Steadman.
23. Five Forks.
24. Appomattox.

Now, comrades, when I have related to you a few incidents of the war which came under my immediate observation, and have stamped themselves indelibly on my mind, I shall give way to some one who will doubtless interest you more than I am able to, speaking in public not being one of my accomplishments.

Before me I see a man whose locks have been silvered by the ruthless march of time. Seeing his face carries me back to the first of July, 1863. He was a boy then, just verging into manhood, brave and strong, a patriot indeed. On yonder hill, back of the Seminary, where the battle waxed warm and the deadly missiles from the well-aimed muskets of the swarming multitude in front, outnumbering us four to one, dealt to our ranks death and destruction on every side, our noble old Colonel, with hundreds of others, had fallen; the remnant of the column was retreating towards the Seminary, and three or four of them, faithful to their old commander, endeavored to carry his lifeless body along; but the enemy was too close. Several of the boys were shot dead while trying to perform this solemn duty. One was left, and seeing the impossibility to accomplish this purpose himself, he unbuckled the Colonel's belt and came off the field, swinging the Colonel's sword, not, however, escaping being wounded; for, as he passed me, the blood was streaming out of his mouth, and the tears down his cheeks. But with the courage of an infuriated lion, he was swearing eternal vengeance on our enemies.

When I was made commander of the regiment, I selected this boy for a position of trust. In every battle after, he was near our colors. At Dabney's Mill the entire color guard and sergeant, with the exception of him, were killed or wounded. I thought they were perhaps exposing themselves needlessly, and I took hold of the colors, intending to look after them myself while the engagement lasted, but this brave boy would not have it so. "Not until I am dead shall any man carry these colors, unless you insist with a peremptory order. Wherever you say, they shall go; but let me carry them until I die." And as "fortune favors the brave," he carried them to the Appomattox.

At the close of the address a roll of those present was made out, and the following survivors answered to their names:

Colonel HORATIO N. WARREN.
1st Lieut. W. L. WILSON, Adjutant.
Corporal BERIAH ORR, Co. A.
Lieutenant D. S. TINSMAN, Co. B.
1st Sergeant J. J. HOFFMAN, Co. C.
Private D. J. HORNER, Co. C.
Private JACOB ZUFAL, Co. C.
Lieutenant N. S. MILLER, Co. D.
1st Sergeant O. P. SHAVER, Co. D.
Private WILLIAM ROGERS, Co. D.
Private HENRY J. MILLER, Co. D.
Private JOHN W. DICKEY, Co. D.
Private J. J. SWANK, Co. D.
Private HARRISON LOHR, Co. D.
Private JOHN H. BISSELL, Co. D.

Sergeant J. V. MILLER, Co. E.
Captain ALBERT HEFFLEY, Co. F.
Lieutenant J. G. GORDILL, Co. F.
Musician C. A. FLATO, Co. F.
Corporal BENJAMIN HAY, Co. F.
Private S. T. FISHER, Co. F.
Private JOSEPH WALKER, Co. F.
Private F. B. COLLINS, Co. F.
Private EDWIN BURCH, Co. G.
Captain GEORGE R. SNOWDEN, Co. I.
Private JERE WALDEN, Co. I.
Private W. J. SHERIFF, Co. I.
Private JAMES E. MACLANE, Co. I.
Lieutenant J. W. DISSINGER, Co. K.
Private JOHN R. DAVIES, Co. K.

Captain Snowden, of Company I, then briefly addressed the veterans, and as he referred in glowing and pathetic terms to the gallant and heroic Colonel Cummins and other brave comrades, who yielded up their lives in the terrible conflict of that bloody field, the tears of this little band of battle-scarred soldiers fell upon the same soil that was made sacred by the blood of their comrades twenty-five years before.

Corporal J. V. Miller, of Company E, Adjutant Wilson and others, also made some appropriate remarks.

One of the objects of the meeting being the location of the site for a monument to the regiment, it was resolved, on motion of Captain Snowden, to place the monument in the front line of the First Corps during the battle of the first day, and that a committee of five, to select the location and style of the same, be appointed. Whereupon the chair announced the following as the committee:

Captain GEORGE R. SNOWDEN, Company I.

Adjutant W. L. WILSON. Sergeant J. V. MILLER, Company E.
Corporal BERIAH ORR, Company A. Private D. J. HORNER, Company C.

On motion, a permanent organization of the regiment was formed, and Colonel Warren was elected permanent President, and Sergeant Hoffman, Secretary and Treasurer.

The place and time for holding the next reunion were then discussed, and finally fixed for Gettysburg, July 1st, 1890.

A cordial invitation was extended to the members of the 121st Regiment to join the regiment at its next reunion.

Representatives of the different companies present were requested to furnish the Secretary with a list of the names and post-office addresses of all the survivors of their respective companies, so that he might be enabled to notify each survivor of the action of this meeting. It was suggested that small contributions be made to defray printing and other necessary expenses, and the sum of $14.60 was placed in the hands of the Treasurer for that purpose.

The little band of soldiers then accompanied the Committee on Monument over the ground the regiment occupied during the first day's fight, and the committee, with the approval of all present, located the monument on the south side of Reynold's Avenue, in a line with, and nearly midway between, the monuments of the 121st and 151st Pennsylvania Volunteers.

The design of the monument will be selected, and the contract for its erection awarded as soon as possible, as it is intended to have it ready for dedication on the 3d of October next.

Before separating it was proposed that the members meet in the Diamond of the town at 4.30 P. M., and join the procession of the Association of the Army of the Potomac, from that point to the National Cemetery, to witness the exercises of the reunion of the " Blue and the Gray."

The meeting then adjourned to July 1, 1890. The utmost harmony and good feeling prevailed throughout, and the occasion was one never to be forgotten by those who participated in this first reunion of the regiment.

JOHN J. HOFFMAN,　　　HORATIO N. WARREN,
　　Secretary.　　　　　　　　　*President.*

SECOND REUNION

HELD AT

GETTYSBURG, SEPTEMBER 11, 1889.

—

ON the afternoon of September 10th, about one hundred of the Survivors of the 142d Pennsylvania Volunteers met in Grand Army Hall, at Gettysburg, to arrange a programme for our Reunion and Dedication to take place September 11th.

The meeting was called to order by the President, Col. H. N. Warren, who in a few timely remarks extended to the comrades a cordial greeting, and then called upon Comrade Brown, of Company H, to lead the audience in singing our national anthem, "My Country 'Tis of Thee," in which all of the veterans heartily participated. This done, remarks were made by Adjutant Wilson, Lieutenant Gilson, Sergeant Hoffman, Captain Heffley, Captain Dushane, and quite a number of the comrades present, when we adjourned to meet and form the regiment at 9 A. M., on the morning of the 11th, on the square in front of the McClellan House, and march to the grove back of the Seminary, and there hold our reunion on the ground made sacred to us all by the many losses we there sustained July 1st, 1863.

At the hour appointed, on the morning of the 11th, the regiment was promptly formed, and nearly two hundred strong marched to the grove in the rear of the Seminary.

Comrade MacLane, of Company I, having brought his camera with him, desired to take a picture of the regiment, which he accomplished satisfactorily after the regiment was thrown into columns by divisions; this ended, the comrades listened to a short history of the regiment, when they voted almost unanimously for the publication of the same.

History of the Regiment by Col. H. N. Warren.

COMRADES: On the afternoon of July 2d, 1888, in this hallowed grove, the first reunion of the 142d Pennsylvania Volunteers was held, and a permanent organization for all of its surviving members entered into. Pursuant to a resolution then adopted, by the providence of an all-wise Ruler, I am here to-day to try and fulfill the requirements of a request of the comrades present upon that occasion, which was to recite to you that might assemble here to-day a short history of the old regiment and the part it took in the suppression of the most gigantic rebellion recorded in history, known as the war of 1861 65.

The regiment was composed of ten companies of Pennsylvania volunteers (see Roster page 63), numbering, all told, officers and men, about 925 able-bodied men. We had all been mustered into the United States service for three years, or during the war, in the month of August, 1862. On the first of September a regimental organization was effected by the choice of the following:

    ROBERT P. CUMMINS, of Somerset County, as Colonel.
    ALFRED B. McCALMONT, of Venango County, as Lieut.-Colonel.
    JOHN BRADLEY, of Lucerne County, as Major.
    W. L. WILSON, of Lucerne County, as Adjutant.
    WILLIAM C. HILLMAN, of Mercer County, as Quartermaster.
    THOMAS J. KEELEY, of Philadelphia, as Surgeon.

On the following day after its organization the regiment was ordered to Washington, arriving there just as the wounded were coming in from the second battle of Bull Run. Few of us had ever seen the distinguished place before, and the dome of the great Capitol building rose up before us in great splendor as we entered the city and helped materially in driving away the gripings with which many of us were afflicted, and which it was quite necessary we should shake off, now that we were approaching the scene where we first expected our valor and courage to be tried. We learned from the wounded, who were flocking into the city, that the Army of the Potomac had been put to flight, and most severely handled on the identical ground where the great struggle in dead earnest first began. Many of these wounded comrades were disheartened, and some demoralized, and we did all we could to inspire them and ourselves with a feeling that victory for our side was not far distant, for we were "coming, Father Abraham, 300,000 strong." Instead of being ordered immediately into battle, as many of us anticipated, we were marched out about four miles near the Maryland line, where we were ordered into camp. Shovels and picks were furnished and soon the whole command was busily engaged throwing up earth-works, the main portion of which was named, when completed, Fort Massachusetts.

We were told that an attack was expected on Washington in our front, and every precaution was used to make our position a formidable one. The first night we were there, after digging hard all day, as commandant of Company A, I was summoned to the Colonel's quarters and informed that I was detailed to take my company and go on picket for the next twenty-four hours; that a regular officer would report shortly and go with and designate to me the line for me to guard. We began to realize then that there was not much play about that kind of soldiering. The officer came and led us out the road about one mile, then helped me station my men so as to cover the road and each side of it about one-third of a mile. I was informed our position was a very important one—that at any moment the cavalry attached to the troops commanded by Stonewall Jackson might dash in and capture my whole force, if we did not keep a sharp look-out, and in case such a thing did occur, and we did not make the necessary resistance to put our forces in the forts and works on their guard, the most serious results might be expected. This was our first picket duty, and, as yet, some of my men scarcely knew how to load a musket, and, while there may not have been an enemy within twenty miles, we could peer out into the darkness in our front and, in our imagination, see long lines of the enemy marching and counter-marching and getting ready to sweep us from the face of the earth. If my memory serves me, most of us were tired and weary, but—sleep! well, we had no use for sleep that evening, the responsibilities of war was crowding in upon us too fast for any of us to think of closing our eyes in slumber. We all wished we had eyes behind as well as in front, so we could see the enemy whichever way he might come, for we were so green we hardly knew what to make of our perilous situation. After we returned to camp and learned how far we were from the enemy, we did not make mention of our perilous service, for until then we supposed we were the outposts nearest the victorious army of Lee.

The next day, while digging in the trenches about this fort, the Army of the Potomac marched out past us into Maryland to meet the enemy at South Mountain and Antietam. They presented anything but an inspiring appearance, their clothes old and dirty and their general make-up tired and careworn from their long marches and recent defeats. We all wondered if that was the glory, or realistic picture we would present after one year in the service of our Uncle Samuel. The head of the column had passed out of our sight about twenty-four hours, when we could hear the distant booming of artillery. We all agreed that "Little Mac," as the boys called him, had either run against a "Sonewall," a "Hill," or had come suddenly upon a barricaded "Longstreet," and, in consequence thereof, was letting loose his "dogs of war." We expected momentarily orders to join them in the shortest possible route and supposed, of course, in our next experience we should realize what it was to participate in a general engagement. Fate, however, decreed otherwise, and at about the end of six days we were ordered to Frederick City, Md., to help care for the wounded from the battle-fields of South Mountain and Antietam, where our army, to a certain extent, had been victorious, though severely punished in accomplishing the same.

We were engaged in this duty about ten days, and were I to spin out and make plain in words the horrible results of these battles, as we saw them and heard of them from the mouths of those that were sent there, shattered and torn in every conceivable shape by bullets and shells (both our friends and our enemies, for from us, in this their non-combative state, they all received the same treatment), I am quite certain that none would disagree with the conclusions we there came to, namely, that war, indeed, was more terrible in its consequences than we had ever before been able to realize. When our next orders came we found our column marching toward Antietam, where we joined the Army of the Potomac, and on the twenty-sixth day of October (which was Sunday and the birthday of your historian), with this grand old army we made our first day's march, and well you must all remember the day, for it never ceased pouring rain from early morning, when we started, until ten o'clock that night, when it changed into sleet and snow, as we halted for the night at the base of a mountain. I might add here that none of us were particularly overjoyed with this our first introduction to actual service. During this night we had half of our men carrying rails with which we made fires to keep warm by and try to dry our clothes. Companies would go out, turn about, and by morning all the rail fences for miles had been appropriated and used up.

The next morning we resumed our march, passing over this barren mountain, and at night camped at Berlin, a short distance from Harper's Ferry. We remained here a day or two and were supplied with rations and forty rounds each of ammunition, and then crossed the Potomac river and started on our long march towards Fredericksburgh, Va. This march was fraught with much that was trying to our experience, for, as yet, our men knew nothing about foraging, little about cooking and less about taking care of and dispensing their rations, so as to spin them out and make them last until another issue. In consequence of this, half of the time we were nearly starved. One instance I remember in my own personal experience that occurred about this time which I will relate: We had been marching hard all day and I was tired and very hungry. Just before halting for the night we passed a house and I stopped and purchased from a Virginia lady two chickens, about the only living things she had left on her farm. She sold them to me, I suppose, because she thought if she did not I would steal them. Well, I had them nicely picked and cleaned, and, though as hungry as a wolf, I determined to keep them for the morrow's march. That evening two friends from an old regiment that had then been in the army nearly a year came over to visit me and see how I was standing the campaign. I had a pleasant visit and was glad of their call and the counsel they gave me. Soon an orderly summoned me to the Colonel's quarters. I excused myself, saying I would be gone but a moment, for them not to go until I returned. I was away possibly ten minutes. When I returned my visitors had gone, and when I looked for my chickens to put them under my head, where I thought would be a save place for them until morning, behold! they had also vanished. This taught me a lesson, and ever after I always knew that if any old soldier friends came to visit me, and I had anything choice in eatables or drinkables, and I wished to keep them, I must double my guard and give instructions to shoot before they challenged.

At one place on this march we halted for a day at a place the boys named Starvation Hollow, and as General Meade rode by our division, the men shouted "crackers and hard-tack" so loud and long at him, in his wrath he ordered the whole division under arms and made them stand in the rain for about two hours. At Berk's Station provisions came up and our hunger was thoroughly appeased. Here we camped for a few days, getting ready for the great battle of Fredericksburgh, Va., which commenced December 13, 1862, in which we were severely chastised, by being compelled to retire from the field with a loss to our regiment of 270 men, killed, wounded and missing. Here, my comrades, let me say, is where our first genuine experience of war commenced—here is where we passed the first ordeal that was calculated to try men's souls—here is where we heard the first rattle of musketry and knew and realized that the leaden missiles, screaming past our ears, coming directly from the muzzles of well-aimed muskets, in the hands of our common enemy, must deal death and destruction to our ranks, and summon many a good friend and comrade to lay his life upon the altar of his country and manfully meet his God.

This battle we lost, and while now we can realize that it was doubtless the will of Almighty God that the encounter should terminate as it did, I have, nevertheless, always felt the blame for the defeat was the result of jealousy and the improper use of the troops composing the left grand division of our army. Had the general commanding the left grand division, with troops which he had in reserve, which were in numbers quite sufficiently adequate, sent to the support of our division, commanded by General Meade, when we charged the enemy and broke their lines, I have no doubt the issue of the entire battle would have been changed, and we should have won a victory. But this was not to be, the troops in reserve were massed on the flats below us, and we were left alone, until forced by a far superior force under Stonewall Jackson to retrace our steps precipitately, and what was left of us formed in rear of our batteries, from which point we had first started to make the charge. Had the reserved divisions of troops followed us, I have no doubt we could have forced the Confederates to have changed their front and thus lose the great advantage of their strong defenses along the Fredericksburgh heights, and with our army, which was in every way splendidly equipped for battle, I believe the day would have been ours.

I need not say to you, comrades, that late that night, when we crossed back over the Rappahannock river, that during our whole term of service of three years and the participation in over a score of hard-fought battles, with all the accessories thereto, I do not recollect of ever feeling so discouraged over the result of anything we ever undertook to do, as I did over the result of this our first engagement.

With an army in active service, soldiers often experience much distress for being obliged to expose themselves unnecessarily to hardships for the good of which they nor any one can see any possible excuse. For example, on this night in December, when we crossed back over the river, it was quite cold and rainy and we were formed in line of battle along the banks of the river and compelled to remain there until late the next morning, instead of being marched up on high land a short distance back from the river, where we could have been more comfortable and escaped the fearful shelling we received from the enemy's batteries on the heights, as soon as daylight dawned and they discovered our position after the retreat we had made during the night. Many times officers in high authority deserved censure for not looking more to the interest of the commands over which they were placed, when from their superiors they received praise, but from the rank and file curses and denunciations, for they knew whereof they spoke.

But I must hasten, for I fear I shall tire you with details which will not interest you, and unless I skip a great deal of our experience, my history will be too long before I shall have occasion to bring you to a point where victory perched on our banners and where the sun, which to us had been dark so long, began to shine with brightness upon our cause, and renew and strengthen our faith in the belief that behind all the dark clouds that had overshadowed us there was a silver lining, and that, sooner or later, the justice of our cause would be vindicated.

The time had now come for us to go into winter quarters, which we did near Belle Plain, Va., and from this time until February nothing of interest occurred, and our time was mostly spent in drill and picket duty. In February a general move was ordered, which also proved a disastrous affair and was known as the Burnside Mud March, and I will pass this by saying that there was enough mud and distress in the four days it occupied to fill a small volume, and when we returned to our quarters our shirts were so nearly alive that when we took them off for a change they nearly walked away. Our next engagement was Chancellorsville, and here we met with further disaster. The general in command, you will remember, issued a windy order, and from its reading one unaccustomed to hearing such orders on the battle-field would have thought the opposing army nearly annihilated, but it turned out, as our men predicted, a delusion that was conceived in close proximity to a canteen of commissary at headquarters. We passed through this battle without much loss. We were making a feint below Fredericksburgh to draw part of the enemy's forces from Chancellorsville, the enemy was shelling us from the heights, when we received word that the 11th Corps had broken and we were ordered to report, with the least possible delay, to the right. As we pulled out, one of the enemy's shells took our Colonel's horse's head off. He was, however, unmolested, except to fall from the horse as the poor animal sank back upon his haunches and soon gave up his life. Another horse was brought up and we moved forward. Before we reached the front at Chancellorsville we had a march of about eighteen miles, and this, I think, without exception, was the hottest march we ever experienced, and I am sure it is no exaggeration to say that twenty-five men dropped dead with sunstroke that afternoon in our corps, and that a man following our column could have walked the first twelve miles and never touched the earth, by reason of the blankets and clothing thrown away by the troops, which it seemed impossible for them to carry, by reason of the terrible heat.

After crossing the river at United States Ford, we passed up to the front, where the battle was raging. The ground had all been fought over and the wounded and dying were crying piteously for help and water. We could not relieve them, for our orders to hurry were positive, and from the roar of the artillery and musketry in front of us, it was evident to us we had arrived at an opportune moment. It was nearly midnight when we wheeled into line, were ordered to fix bayonets and to go in with a yell. This was a place to try the mettle of any command, but there was no faltering. Every one of us had made up our minds to do our best and take the consequences. Just as we expected the word forward, there came a lull in the battle and by mutual consent both armies ceased firing, and instead of going in with a yell, we quietly laid down on our bayoneted muskets until daylight.

The next morning the battle was resumed, and all day, as it would rage, first on the right, then left or center, it seemed to be about an even match or draw game. That night rain came down in torrents, the river commenced swelling and the mud deepening, and, I suppose, the general commanding thought he had better get his army back nearer his supply base, before the elements made his chances for a withdrawal an impossiblity. Again we find ourselves discouraged and our numbers wonderfully depleted, another great battle fought and no seeming advantage gained. We then went into camp below Fredericksburgh, about one mile from the Rappahannock, arranging our picket line along its banks facing the enemy's pickets on the opposite bank of the stream. Here doubtless some of you may recollect of swimming over the river in the night and trading coffee for tobacco, as this was about the first opportunity of this kind that our boys had. About this time quite a number of the New York volunteers' time expired and many returned to their homes ; and while the government at Washington was sending new relays of men as fast as they could, it seemed to us for awhile that our army was growing weaker, which was anything but encouraging. We, nevertheless, were kept drilling and preparing for another grand movement, which we knew could not be far in the future. Presently all was commotion, orders were issued for several days' rations, forty rounds of ammunition, and to be ready to move at a moment's notice. Complying with this we soon found ourselves moving at a lively pace towards Washington. A rumor was afloat that General Lee with his entire army by a forced march was forty-eight hours ahead of us, making up the Shenandoah Valley with the probable intention of pushing the seat of war into Pennsylvania, to give the Yankees a taste of the medicine that Virginia had been swallowing for two long and bloody years.

' Our corps, the first, commanded by General Reynolds, by long and hard marching up through Virginia and Maryland, reached the Pennsylvania line near Gettysburg on the night of June 30th. The scouts and cavalry reported the enemy in force at Gettysburg, distant from us about eight miles ; how large a force it was impossible to tell, but early, July 1st, we were in motion headed for Gettysburg, and as the men were completely jaded and worn out by their long march, the whisperings that we would doubtless meet the enemy that day and contest their further advance into the Keystone State, was received by the men and officers with more gratification than to have learned we had another long and tedious day's march to perform. We were then nearly twelve hours in advance of the balance of the army ; nevertheless, our General Reynolds determined to give battle, and trust to Providence for the consequences, and you will remember that his life was one of the first sacrifices we had to make, as he fell while riding forward with the advance skirmishers feeling the enemy's position, and thus ended his great war record as he expired in the arms of that faithful soldier, Adjutant-General Major Beard, as he happened to be near him when the fatal bullet from the enemy's sharp-shooters accomplished its deadly mission.

As we came into line on Seminary Ridge, we were joined by a citizen whose locks were silvered by many winters, and, armed with a squirrel rifle, he was full of patriotism and fight, and when the battle opened did good and faithful service with our men. We afterwards learned his name was John Burns, who was the only citizen of the place or vicinity who took an active part in the engagement, and we all felt proud of our old hero, whose name afterwards became famous in song and verse because of his distinguished service on this field of battle.

General Doubleday succeeded General Reynolds in command, and the preparation for the action went on as if nothing had occurred to mar its progress—skirmishing and artillery firing seemed to be the order of the day, for two or three hours—when the enemy about three o'clock in the afternoon began to show a bolder front, and presently pushed out of the woods into the open field on Seminary Ridge, with two long lines of infantry, outflanking us by nearly one-third of a mile, and we had but one line of battle and no reserves. We fought them for a short time, our men never flinching, except as they were mowed down by the terrible fire from front and flank, and then in sheer desperation we were ordered to charge, which we did, but were repulsed, and the remnant of the line that was left rallied round the brick Seminary, and there fought until we were nearly surrounded by the superior number that swarmed from every direction. Our men at this point used their muskets until, by fast firing, they became so hot they were compelled to drop them, when they would take the one nearest them on the ground, rendered useless because the owner of it was dead ; and, I will add here, there was no scarcity of muskets, as the dead and wounded were largely in the majority of our regiment. Here we were compelled to leave the lifeless bodies of many of our loved comrades. Notably conspicuous among that number was our brave, loyal and much-beloved Col. R. P. Cummins and Acting Adjutant Tucker, for, as the enemy seemed to outnumber us four to one, it was apparent that unless we retreated down the hill and through the town we must all be captured. This we did in as orderly a manner as the circumstances would permit, and when we reached the Seminary on the opposite side of the town, we formed a line of battle among the monuments and grave-stones, and once more faced the enemy. When the battle began our corps numbered something over 9,000 and now only about 2,500 were left. That night our regiment mustered seventy-five men and three officers—when we commenced the battle we numbered about 320 men and sixteen officers; so while we were forming our broken lines we realized we had been very severely punished, though we were not disheartened, for the balance of our army began to pour in and we made the night hideous by our yells of joy because of their opportune arrival.

General Meade had been put in command of the army, and arrived that night in time to form his lines from Culp's Hill to Round Top Mountain, which position was the key-note to our success the two days following. The fighting for the two next days was simply beyond description. The fact that on both sides there were on that field nearly 50,000 killed and wounded soldiers, places Gettysburg as the greatest battle of the war; and as we were victorious on the third day, and on the morning of the fourth day General Grant marched into Vicksburg, we recognize this time as the point in the war when the backbone of the rebellion began to weaken and the doctrine of secession lost its grip.

I might relate many hairbreadth escapes by our officers and men, some of whom, by the kind providence of an all-wise God, were spared, and are yet numbered among our best and most enterprising citizens. One I recollect in my company, Lieutenant F. M. Powell, whose faithful Bible, carried in a side-pocket nearly over his heart, saved his life, and there are many others living to-day who, upon that occasion, were captured by the enemy and whose bones now would doubtless be mouldering in the hot soil adjacent to the prison-pens of Andersonville, had it not been for the hasty retreat made by the enemy, thus affording many of our men an opportunity to make good their escape.

Here let me mention the names of two of our brave and efficient officers: Captain J. M. Dushane of Company H, and Captain Albert Heffley of Company F, who we sadly missed: both were captured and too closely guarded by their captors to make good their escape. They returned to us after the lapse of many months somewhat diminished in weight, by reason of their experiences in southern prisons, but as fervent and loyal in spirit as ever. And, my comrades, I rejoice with you, that I see both their smiling faces with us to-day, which proves to us that some men in the 142d were proof against rebel bullets, starvation, imprisonment, vermin, and all the accessories of those places, calculated to lure the monster Death and make him thrice welcome.

And there were scores of others, whose bright young lives, by the fortunes of this great battle, were brought to an untimely end. They are not forgotten, for every year, on the thirtieth day of May, their comrades who still live, together with all patriotic citizens, meet and plant fresh flowers on their graves, that the noble sacrifice made by them for their country may be kept fresh and green in the hearts of a grateful republic.

We are now, my comrades, on the historic field of Gettysburg, with its thousands of weary men, thousands of wounded and thousands of dead. Victory is inscribed on our banners, yet before we push out in pursuit of the enemy we have a sad duty to perform, bury our dead hastily and render our wounded such comfort and help as we are able to do with the circumstances which surround us. This accomplished and we find our column again in motion, headed, as we supposed, towards the nearest point on the Potomac, towards which the enemy is pushing with all the speed possible, to effect a crossing, if he can, before the falling rain swells the stream to such dimensions that will make it impossible for him to cross. As we look around us and see the terrible results of this battle, with about 50,000 killed and wounded men, and horses without number slain and lying where they fell, no burials of any kind having been made since the battle commenced on the first day, naturally our hearts are filled with sadness, and the officers and men of each company devise all the means in their power to render some assistance to our wounded, and to bury our dead comrades with as much respect and love as it is possible for us to show them under the existing circumstances. Visiting Seminary Ridge, where we were first engaged on the morning of the first, we find our dead lying where they fell, and their upturned faces black from the burning rays of the scorching sun, so that it was with much difficulty we were enabled to distinguish one from the other.

We were soon called from this sorrowful duty with the information that our column would soon be moving. Towards evening rations were furnish and a large supply of ammunition, orders to march promulgated, and we are heading to a point on the Potomac nearest to our present location, towards which it was thought the enemy was hastening, so as to successfully accomplish a crossing before being overtaken by our pursuing columns. After marching about forty-eight hours, as fast as it was possible to lead troops in the condition we were after passing through so terrible a battle, there came down upon us from the angry clouds above the most drenching rain I ever witnessed, either before, during or since the war. We were, at the time, on a stone pike leading into a small place called Funkstown, Maryland, where there was a small, but deep and sluggish, stream of water, spanned by a stone bridge. As we crossed the bridge, there was opened in our front quite a sharp skirmish fire, which made the men and horses in the command prick up their ears, and the men to examine their guns and see that they were in a reliable condition. The old caps from the tubes they removed and substituted new ones, so as to be in readiness for the enemy, who, from all appearances, was prepared to give us a warm reception, in case we continued our advance in that direction. As soon as we reached the other side of the stream, hearing the command, "On the right by file into line," it was unnecessary to say to the men, "The enemy is not far away. If you are in the habit of calling upon anyone higher than yourself for protection, when perils surround you, you had better embrace the immediate opportunity of doing so, for we shall soon pass through that wheat-field stubble in our front and will doubtless receive from the enemy a shower of lead that will compare favorably with the shower of rain through which we have just come, except it will be much more effective in destroying life and in making us feel and realize more fully the uncertainties of each coming hour."

The line now formed, we look for the word "Forward," but it is not forthcoming, and the men conclude it is only a scare, and instinctively they commence gathering a few rails and bits of wood, with which to build small fires, dry themselves a little and make a hot cup of coffee, but as the preliminaries of this are being accomplished, a shell comes tearing and hissing just above our heads, and each man, without orders or suggestions, secures his musket and resumes his position in the line. The skirmish line is run forward, two or three batteries push to the front, their horses on the dead run. As they reach a good position they wheel into battery and open a lively fire. We push forward to their support, and in a moment observe the enemy have fortified their position with a good line of earth-works. The cavalry to our right and our skirmish line, with its reinforcement, now almost a line of battle, open a lively fire, the shells and bullets are flying round us promiscuously. Our men in line cannot fire, so they tear down the fences in front and rear of us, pile them in line in front of the batteries, then with spades, picks, bayonets and everything they can work with, we, in twenty minutes, have an earth-work that we should be pleased to have the enemy try to take. This, however, they do not propose to try, and after we have exhausted every ingenuity to get them out of their works to an attack on ours, so hastily thrown up, or to an open-field combat, with no success, we are ordered forward and succeed in taking their line of works, but find only a few pickets in them, the main portion of their men having been withdrawn under the cover of the woods, leaving only a few to make as big a showing as possible and thus give them time to cross the river. Some portions of our army were pushed forward to the river, arriving in time to capture and make prisoners a portion of their rearguard, consisting of about 2,500 men all told, General Lee having successfully crossed the swollen stream in safety with the main body of his entire army, leaving only the badly wounded and killed for us to care for. We soon crossed the river at a point nearer Washington and guarded the gaps in the Blue Ridge Mountains, through which it was thought if General Lee were allowed to pass, in the absence of nearly all the troops from the defenses about the Capital, he might dash in, and, in spite of his defeat, become master of the situation. Sabbath came and we were massed about one mile from Thoroughfare Gap, where we were allowed a day of rest. That Sunday morning service was held, and general thanksgiving to Almighty God, who had given us the victory, went up from all our hearts. Our entire division was massed in a small grove of natural timber located near where we were stationed. As we did not know what a moment might bring forth, we marched to the grove with all of our appurtenances of battle, and listened to one of the most eloquent discourses it was ever my pleasure to give ear to, and, I might further add, that in my recollection I never beheld a more devout assemblage of worshipers.

That night, shortly after dark, quite an uproar was caused by a dash of three or four hundred of Stewart's cavalry through our strong picket line, and down almost in our very midst, they not knowing what they were running into, and we not knowing what was coming. At short notice, however, our men were in line with fixed bayonets, ready for any emergency, and it was with much difficulty we could restrain our men from opening a heavy fire upon the mob in our immediate front, which we desired to obviate on account of the heavy line of pickets of our own, which were all mixed up in the darkness with the enemy, all of whom were cursing, yelling, firing and fighting in a most desperate manner. We soon organized a strong skirmish line and pushed them forward and strengthened up our picket line, the enemy's cavalry, all that were not captured, flying back through the mountain pass faster than they came through when they made the attack.

We remained here but a short time, when we pushed on towards the Rappahannock river. Lee, in the meantime, had reached and was occupying his defenses along the Fredericksburgh side of the stream. Here we camped for some time and recruited up our tired animals and filled up our depleted ranks. Soon our camps were laid out in regular order, drill of every kind commenced, and a general reorganization of the entire army entered into. This was no sooner accomplished than occasional sorties by our cavalry, supported by small bodies of infantry, would be sent over the river and out into the enemy's lines as far as it was thought expedient to go. Once or twice we crossed the river on these errands.

Late in the fall the enemy abandoned this line of defenses and fell back across the Rapidan river and occupied and entrenched themselves on the opposite high banks of this stream, we pushing forward to Culpepper and into winter quarters, with our picket line confronting the enemy's along the aforesaid river a distance of three to four miles from our camps. Nothing occurred to mar our peace from this time until the spring of 1864, when we entered upon the Wilderness campaign.

I forgot to mention that previous to crossing the Rappahannock, after the balance of the army had crossed, our division was taken to guard the Orange and Alexandria Railroad from above Manassas to the Rappahannock, and that Moseby's men kept us in hot water most of the time for about six weeks, keeping us constantly on the alert to prevent their depredations, and having us in line of battle ready for action sometimes four or five times during one night, so that when we were relieved and ordered to the front with the rest of our corps we were all rejoiced.

On the third day of May the Wilderness campaign commenced. When we went into winter quarters late the fall previous, your historian was promoted to major and left in command of the regiment, Lieut.-Colonel McCalmont having been detailed to take command of Camp Curtin. During the winter we drilled nearly every day in company, in skirmish and battalion drill, and we thought by this time we were well up in all that it took to make good soldiers; in fact our whole army was in fine condition and splendid discipline, and when, after every preparation had been made for a long and active campaign, the order was issued for the Army of the Potomac to move, with General Meade as its immediate commander, and General Grant the commander of all the forces, with his headquarters with the headquarters of our army, we pushed out with confidence, but with the firm belief that there was a campaign before us the magnitude of which would overshadow all previous undertakings, but through which, if we came out alive, we could reasonably hope for a victory that would vouchsafe to the American people a peace which would be as lasting and glorious as the terrible price of blood and treasure with which it had been purchased was, in magnitude, greater than any pen or words could describe.

In this we were not mistaken, for after the morning we crossed the Rapidan river, for a little over one year, there was scarcely a day we were not under some kind of a fire, and from the first shot in the Wilderness until late in the winter, around Petersburgh, there was no cessation of hostilities, and all through the winter, in fact, there was scarcely a day we were not exchanging shot and shell with the enemy some place along our line. Our first engagement in this campaign was the Wilderness, where, for forty hours, without a break or a rest, the battle raged with unabated fury.

On the night of the second we moved towards Spottsylvania. All night we plodded along, feeling our way. At daybreak, having made a distance of only about four miles, we were halted and ordered to make coffee in as short a time as it was possible to do so, for just in front of us there appeared a small force of the enemy's cavalry, which seemed inclined to dispute our further progress in that direction. We were told that to dispose of them would only be a breakfast spell for us, after we had drank our hot coffee. This place we named Laurel Hill. As soon as we had our coffee, we went forward in line of battle. As we advanced the cavalry disputed our way, but fell back as our heavy line of skirmishers began pouring into them a sharp and decisive fire. Presently, however, there emerged from the woods a heavy line of the enemy's infantry and a battery on each flank, which opened fire on our advancing column and caused the brigade on our right to break, leaving our right flank entirely without protection. This compelled us to fall back across a field to a thicket of woods, where we rallied and in a few moments, with logs and fences, threw up a breastwork from which they did not try to dislodge us, preferring, we supposed, to have us try and take a similar work which they had constructed before we came up. Each side strengthened their position until the next night, with no heavy firing on either side, except by the artillery, the skirmishers and sharp-shooters, who kept up a constant fire, each making their opponents in line, and everywhere in range, as uncomfortable as it was in their power to do.

The second night here, about ten o'clock, we received orders to advance over our works, and our division was formed in five lines, about thirty feet apart, with orders for all to remove the caps from their guns, except the front line. Here our regiment exhibited a coolness so commendable that it is deserving of especial mention. When the lines were formed we found ourselves in the rear line. The enemy had evidently, in some way, learned of our intended charge upon their works, for they had the woods enfiladed with artillery, and before the order to go forward had been issued to us, they opened upon us a most destructive fire, fairly cutting the trees down over our heads, and filling the entire woods with hissing and bursting shells. The lines in front of us became panic-stricken and ran back over us and back into the works. Our line was cool and we moved forward and took the advance, the officers of the other lines rallied their men and formed them in our rear, and soon the order to move forward was promulgated. Our men had fixed bayonets and put the caps again on their muskets and forward we went with a yell. We succeeded in getting within about fifty feet of their works, when it seemed as if a solid sheet of fire from the enemy's muskets made it utterly impossible for us to advance another foot. The supporting lines all went back. We remained in this death-trap, covering as best we could behind trees and logs, until we received orders to withdraw as quietly as we could, the pickets a little behind us having by this time been reinforced and strengthened their pits by digging and with such logs as they could lay hold of.

One incident I recollect, in this advance, which, at the time, made me very proud of the old 142d. A shell exploded in a regiment just to our left and front—in the line ahead of us. The shell must have killed and maimed nearly a score of men, and the regiment sprang to their feet and went back like a lot of cattle that had been stampeded. I gave the command, "Attention, 142d! forward, left oblique march!" and they filled up the place as nicely as they could have done it on drill in a quiet camp, without a man ever flinching or murmuring his disapproval of the performance. Each man, like myself, seemed to realize the necessity of a compact line, if we hoped for success.

The woods here were afire, and many of our wounded were

burned to death, and when all was over and we landed behind our works once more, there were more than one of us expressed our thanks that we were alive and out of that place, which reminded us more of the infernal regions than any place we had yet had occasion to visit. After fighting here over the works for about two days, we move to the left and find ourselves in line at Spottsylvania, in a miserable swamp. Here we whiled away about two days in deadly combat, and which was about a draw game, except that the Second Corps gained a march on the enemy by the capture of nearly 8,000 prisoners in a single haul, which, of course, crippled them to quite an extent. Our losses in this battle were heavy, and our men by this time were so tired and weary, that when they were under a heavy fire in supporting a line, not being able to fire themselves, they would lie down and sleep as soundly as you could wish, though every few moments some of them would be wounded and others shot dead while unconscious of everything around them. After the capture of the large number of prisoners, the enemy fell back about half a mile to another line of earth-works they had constructed, and in the morning surveying the scene inside the works they abandoned was enough to make a strong man's heart sick, for there were wounded men lying under those that were dead —they were literally piled on top of each other and presented a lamentable sight. That night as I was walking from one end of the regiment to the other to keep a sufficient number of my men awake so as be ready to fill up the line in our immediate front, in case it became demoralized or exhausted, as they were keeping up a heavy firing, I extended my walk to possibly one hundred feet to the right of the regiment to examine the lay of the ground, and was contemplating taking the regiment out of this miserable swamp, if I could do so without endangering the front line.

It was about midnight and very dark, and a drizzling rain was making us cold and uncomfortable, and we were receiving the enemy's fire which we could not return, and I was desirous of improving our surroundings if it was possible. I had either lost my rubber coat or some one had taken it without leave or license, and I was beginning to feel the need of it very much; and, as I pushed my way through the darkness, I stumbled over a man lying flat on his back and covered with a good gum blanket. It was here, I think, I had the most solemn soliloquy of my life, feeling cold and wet and not well pleased on account of the loss of my gum coat. The selfish idea of making my loss good by the capture of this blanket was not long forming, and I reached down and carefully pulled it off from my unknown comrade, who, I thought, was taking a comfortable snooze ; after doing so, it occurred to me that my friend might be dead, so I touched his forehead and was at once convinced that his troubles were all over, for he was cold and still in death. Then came my soliloquy. I was about one hundred feet to the right of our regiment, all alone except the dead who were thickly scattered all around me ; it was midnight, and I was about to rob a dead comrade of his covering. Was it right? After mature deliberation, I decided it was, and took the blanket and made good use of it until morning and the rain had ceased.

We were soon ordered to move again by the left flank, and to leave a heavy picket line in our front, but not to communicate to them the orders we had received. We thought it was good-by to the boys we were leaving, for we were satisfied as soon as the enemy learned of our withdrawal they would push vigorously for their capture. I left the men in charge of a tried and brave officer, and so expert had they, themselves, become in looking out for themselves under the most trying circumstances, that I was satisfied that if any of our picket line succeeded in getting away, when the enemy found we were gone and they pushed for their capture, our men would, for they had become very proficient, and knew just how to take every advantage that presented itself, whether they were advancing or retreating. And that evening my confidence in them was verified, for every man reported ; all tired and weary, but in good spirits and full of jokes over the long running fight they had all day with the enemy, who had vigorously pursued and tried to capture them. During the day we had marched by the left flank after the retreating enemy without any very serious interruptions, and concluded that we were making good headway towards Richmond.

Once, however, by reason of the stubbornness of the enemy's rear-guard, who sent us their compliments in the shape of shell and solid shot from their rearmost battery, we were forced into line of battle at Tolopotomy Creek, and our brigade pushed forward in line of battle for nearly a mile through the fields and woods. The result of which was the capture of about 100 tired-out Confederates, a cow and calf, some pigs, chickens and a barn full of tobacco. When we came back into the road each man was well provided with tobacco, and not a few of them had succeeded in providing themselves with enough poultry so that their messes that evening enjoyed a good, square meal of something that varied from the ordinary rations of our every-day living That night we slept in line of battle and were not aroused until early morn by the bugle, which warned us that we would soon again be on the move, and if any breakfast was to be partaken of, only a few moments would be tolerated for that purpose.

We were soon again on the march, and kept it up all day until just dusk, when we came to the North Anna river. The enemy in small numbers were there to dispute our crossing, but when a few guns from our artillery opened on them and a heavy line of skirmishers advanced and gave them a few rounds, they abandoned the ford and ran for the woods. Our pontoons were soon down and we were pouring across as fast as we could march. No enemy in sight, and it was nearly dark, our conclusions were that we would soon halt for the night, and as the idea prevailed, all of the cooks, drum corps and pack horses of the different regiments were up and the men in line. Many of them had picked up rails and were carrying them so as to be ready to kindle fires quickly, as soon as we halted, and make coffee and prepare what they had for their evening meal. We had closed up our ranks and were marching in fours, expecting every moment the head of the column would halt, when, to the utter astonishment of all present, the enemy in a good solid line of battle emerged from the woods but a short distance from us, and commenced pouring into our ranks the most murderous infantry fire I ever witnessed. Our line for a few moments became almost panic-stricken, and went back towards the river at as lively a pace as I had ever seen them move. While doing so our batteries were tearing across the pontoons, and as soon as they reached the top of the river's bank, they were ordered into line, our men rallied around them and such a battle, for about one hour, I think we never saw during our whole term of service. A sheet of flame from our batteries and muskets not only checked the advancing enemy from driving us in the river, but sent them back over that field with as great, or greater, loss than we ourselves had sustained, which, I will assure you, was heavy for the number of men engaged.

You will recollect in this pasture-field there was a small stream of water which a man could easily leap over, but which had cut a channel four to six feet in depth, and which, at this time, contained very little water. When we retreated towards the river some of our men dropped in this natural place of protection, so closely were we pursued, and remained there hugging the banks. And the enemy passed over them, when pushing towards the river and back over them, when we in turn drove them back. It is needless for me to say to you that the boys that did this were much rejoiced at their narrow escape from a trip to some Southern prison.

After this very sharp engagement we advanced our lines about half a mile and built works, where, for twenty-four hours, we engaged the enemy in a most bitter sharp-shooting and skirmish duel. It was almost sure death to a man to expose himself on either side, for each side seemed in bad humor and kept up an incessant fire at anything they saw resembling man or beast. After about forty-eight hours of this incessant unpleasantness, late at night we withdrew from this position, by the left flank, as usual, and early the next morning we found ourselves facing the same old enemy at Cold Harbor. Here they seemed to be in a terrible frame of mind and fought like wild cats. The losses in some of the new regiments in this battle, who were not accustomed to the bushwhacking warfare we had been engaged in for about three weeks, was simply terrible. The new regiments of heavy artillery that joined our army here, and were, by necessity, armed and used as infantry, were simply mowed down by the hundred, and fell and were swept to the earth almost like you have seen grain fall before the reaper. We hear that our watchword, "On to Richmond," was nearly realized, that we were only about four miles from the doomed city, and we rejoiced in the belief that the city and Lee's whole force must soon succumb to the continued bull-dog persistence of our commander, General Grant, who, by this time, had given us to understand, and fully believe, that there would be no let up or cessation of hostilities until the desired end had been accomplished. However, after a hard battle, each side fortified and fought over the works for about one week in the most malignant style either could invent, and many were killed on both sides.

Late on a rainy night we stole away from our enemies and hurriedly marched through the Chickahominy Swamp, and to the James river, which we crossed at City Point in transports which had been sent there for that purpose. Here we heard our destination was Petersburgh, Va., which we were to capture, and thus cut off the supplies to Richmond by rail, which, of necessity, must come through there. In case we were successful, we readily comprehended that the enemy, with their supplies cut off, must, of necessity, abandon their capital, which they had so gallantly defended for three long and bloody years.

We were told that if we did not make a forced march that General Butler and his division would capture the city before we arrived, and we would thus be cheated out of a large share of the glory of the campaign. Our men, not inclined, however, to credit all the rumors regarding Butler's achievements, were not at all astonished when, after marching hard through dust and sand nearly a foot deep all day, and arriving very late that night to a position as near to Petersburgh as the enemy seemed inclined to have us come, we were halted in line of battle and ordered to rest for the night on our arms, ready for an attack at any moment, as the skirmishers in our front were keeping up a lively exchange of compliments, and it was not known what an hour might bring forth.

This march from City Point to the place we rested that night was the dustiest march we ever experienced. Clouds of dust rolled up and nearly suffocated men and horses every step of the way. In the morning, after we had made our coffee and everything was in readiness, we advanced. This was the eighteenth of June, 1864. By one o'clock we had driven the enemy about one mile in a fair, open-field engagement, and had forced them back into their last line of works around Petersburgh. During this afternoon the 142d crowned herself with glory, in one particular move, which is deserving of especial mention. We were advancing and our position was in the center, if I recollect right, of the second line of battle, the lines being about ten rods apart. The enemy was pushed out of a woods into an open field, our front line marching forward and firing, and the enemy returning the fire, but falling back. General Chamberlain, commanding our brigade, noticing that his front line was shorter than the enemy's—about a regiment—dispatched an aid with orders to me to double-quick the 142d and form them on the right of the front line. I gave the command to the regiment and we moved double-quick, leaving the line we were in, and when we were sufficiently away from them, moved by the right flank and then by the left and formed, joining the right of the front line, and our men opened fire and moved right along, firing with the front line, until we had driven the enemy, as I said before, into their last line of works. The movement was made just as coolly and almost with as much precision as it would have been done in drill, and our regiment was highly commended for its beautiful performance.

At this point there was a hill over which the enemy had gone, and through a ravine, and on top of the opposite bank of this ravine, about fifty feet back, was situated their last line of works, into which they had taken refuge, and which were bristling with artillery, the guns in our front being twenty to forty feet apart. We were ordered to lie down and cover under this hill, which we did, the enemy not able to reach us. For a little while we felt quite secure from any damage they were able to inflict upon us from their works.

Soon regimental commanders were summoned to brigade headquarters, at the right of the line. We were told that the line of works on the opposite side of the ravine were the last around Petersburgh, and at three o'clock the whole army was ordered to charge, and it was thought we would capture the city and Lee's army. We were highly complimented for our morning's work, and told to inform all of the line officers of the programme for three o'clock, and for them in turn to tell their men, and for all to peek over the hill and take in, as well as possible, the situation, in order to do what we did intelligently. This was novel to us, for we had been fighting from the Wilderness to this place, with little or no knowledge as to the exact object to be attained, and this new order of things rather captivated the officers and men, and, though they could see before them a desperate undertaking, when the order came at three o'clock our line responded to a man and went forward with an enthusiasm hardly ever witnessed in battle.

Our brigade the day before had been strengthened by a new regiment, the 187th Pennsylvania Volunteers, numbering about 850 men, and this was their first battle. There were four old regiments, including the 142d, and this new regiment made a line covering about the same distance the four old ones did. General Chamberlain ordered the old troops to go forward in the front line and that the supporting line, composed of the new regiment, should follow us at a distance of about 150 feet. He informed us that he and his staff would be between the two lines for any further instructions we might require. His orders to us was to watch the brigades on our right and left, and in case they broke and did not succeed in carrying the works, for us not to go too far and be captured, but if, as far as we could see, all went well, he would be pleased to have us on top of the enemy's works just a little in advance of our neighbors on the right and left.

At three o'clock the order was given, and our men dashed over the brow of the hill and down through the ravine, every man yelling at the top of his voice, to give as much enthusiasm as possible to the charge and thus terrify the enemy. Going through the ravine our men scattered like sheep, but coming up the bank of the ravine every man was in his place in a solid line and anxious to push for the works, which were situated about forty to sixty feet back. The enemy poured a terrific fire from the works, but most of it passed over our heads and caught the line that was our support. We looked to our right and left, and the brigades in both had broken and were retreating in disorder to the position from whence they had started. We looked back, and no supporting line was in sight, and no general and staff for further directions, and just here the enemy opened a galling fire of grape and canister down the ravine, cutting everything to pieces just in the rear of us. We ordered our men to lie down and hug the hill, and open up a fire in front and keep the enemy down in their works, which they did successfully.

The officer commanding the 149th, on our right, very shortly crept along the hill and we together held a very hurried council of war. He ranked me about ten days, and I naturally appealed to him for directions. After a short deliberation, we concluded, as our men were holding the line down in our front, we would together run the gauntlet of this ravine and see if we could find out what was wrong, and also to get further instructions what to do. This we did, and found our supporting line had been cut nearly to pieces, our general had been carried off mortally wounded, and every part of the line but ours had been repulsed. Just then an aid came up from corps headquarters with the general's compliments for our charge, and with instructions for us to hold every inch of ground we had taken, but not to attempt to go into the works alone. With these instructions, after giving this new regiment (which was somewhat dazed with the rough usage they had received) advice what they should do, we each took two spades and charged again through the ravine to our regiments, both escaping the storm of grape and canister with which the enemy was sweeping this ravine from works further to their right, where their line angled and gave them a fine position with their artillery to make this ravine a very unhealthy locality.

As soon as we arrived we gave each regiment a spade, and while part of the men kept up a constant fire in their front, the rest were busy digging pits about thirty feet apart. In doing this they used their bayonets, their hands and everything they could make available, and with the help of this one spade to each regiment, by dark we had pits in good shape and large enough to hold six to ten men each, and from which our men were instructed to keep up a constant fire on anything they saw move in their front. So vigilant were they that neither the infantry nor artillery in our front could fire a shot at them without running the risk of certain death.

We remained here until three o'clock next morning, when our line was withdrawn, leaving our pits well filled with men, with a large supply of cartridges sufficient to last them until dark the next evening, when they would be relieved. We were instructed to retire across the ravine as quietly as possible and build a line of works on the brow of the hill from which we charged. This we did and found it very laborious, as the soil was hard clay and very dry, and if we had not known that in the morning, as soon as the enemy discovered the earth-works, we would get a good shelling, I doubt, with the men's weariness, if we would have been able to perform this duty; but we accomplished it, and by daylight we had our breastworks good and secure, and while the enemy, as we expected, opened upon us very vigorously, they could do us very little damage, and while they were wasting their powder and shell our men rested, and most of them slept, being very much fatigued from our previous forty-eight hours' overexertion.

From this position we were soon relieved by the Ninth Corps, from which command a regiment of miners dug under and mined the enemy's fort and works. From this advanced position they kept the pits we dug that day, after further strengthening them, full of men and kept them firing constantly for six weeks. The miners of the regiment at the same time were tunneling under their fort and works, which were, at the end of this time, blown up, burying a battery of artillery and quite a number of men. This was known as "Burnside's Mine." We moved to the left when relieved, extending our lines in that direction.

Our next important work was building a fort, which was named Fort Hell. Here our lines were exceedingly close to the enemy, our pickets being only about fifty feet in front of our works, and the enemy's pickets so close that they could easily talk to each other. After the engineers staked this fort, our regiment, with a detail from some of the other regiments in the brigade, amounting to about 300 men in all, were the first to commence the work, and as I had charge of the work the first night I recollect how careful we were not to make any undue noise for fear of informing the enemy what we were at. The work was pushed with great vigor, but much caution, until we had a ditch about six feet wide and as many deep excavated, and the dirt thoroughly packed in an embankment. This we accomplished by morning, and were prepared for a good shelling, which we duly received at daybreak, when the enemy first discovered the work we were prosecuting, but by this time their shells did not to any extent molest us, and the work of strengthening the fort was continued for a week or more until we thought them almost impregnable. After this the regiment furnished a good detail each day to help dig the wagon-way, which was made from the rear about a mile up to and along the lines, for the purpose of protecting the transportation of stores and ammunition coming up to the front. It was a work of great magnitude, but saved many lives, as there was scarcely an hour in any day when a vigorous shelling was not kept up some place along the line.

Soon after this Burnside's Mine was exploded. The lines all along for about five miles were in readiness at 4 A. M., and when the torch was lighted which blew up the mine, all the artillery, numbering several hundred guns, and all the infantry with their muskets let loose at one time. It made a lively commotion among our enemies, who, with the exception of their picket, were quietly sleeping. Had a charge been made right away after this bombardment and tremendous volley, I have no doubt Petersburgh and the entire Army of Northern Virginia under Lee would have been captured, for the ground shook for miles around almost as if an earthquake had taken place, and prisoners which we took afterwards informed us that on that morning for a few moments their entire line was paralyzed with fear lest they should all be hurled in the air and buried in a similar way to those in the fort that was blown up. The charge, however, was for some reason delayed, and when it was made proved more disastrous than otherwise.

The enemy shortly after this were detected mining one of our forts, and the guns from this fort were removed and wooden ones substituted and a similar fort erected in the rear with the regular guns placed therein. For about one week we were kept constantly under arms, so as to be ready for them when they should decide to blow it up.

They selected the afternoon for this performance, and as soon as they applied the match which was calculated to turn this fortification upside down, and bury everything in it, they jumped over their works for a charge. Almost instantly our guns opened on them from all along the line, and they were hurled back with heavy loss and in much confusion. Owing to mismanagement of their mine the explosion under our fort was nothing but a fizzle, the packing in the entry under the fort being badly put in, and the force of the explosion was, to a great extent, spent in hurling the dirt back through the entry toward their own lines.

Shortly after this occurrence we were relieved, and again moving by the left flank. We heard our corps had been selected to take the Weldon Railroad, and thus cut off a source of their supplies. We marched, I should think, about two miles when the skirmishers were sent out, and our brigade being in advance we were formed in two lines of battle for the charge. We were in the second line, and your obedient servant, being the senior officer in the three regiments comprising the second line, was placed in charge of the line. These preliminaries accomplished we pushed forward out of the woods into an open field. Here we espied on the opposite side of the field, and along the railroad, a line of the enemy's cavalry drawn up, and as we emerged from the woods they gave us a volley from their carbines. "Fix bayonets!" and "Charge!" ran along the line, and in no time we were going forward yelling, the first line discharging their muskets as they ran.

The cavalry did not wait to shake hands with us, but made off, except a few that were unsaddled and killed, and we had possession of the road. The front line passed over the road and halted. We came up, and fearing we might be driven back, the balance of our corps not yet being in sight with our line, we proceeded to make our charge of some account. We stacked arms and our line advanced, and each man took hold of the rails and ties and overturned them twice, then took the ties and iron and made a good breastwork. That night the enemy tried hard to dislodge us, and came very nearly accomplishing it, but were finally repulsed. We continued to strengthen our position, and the Sunday morning following the enemy in large numbers made a very determined effort to retake the road, but failed.

In this battle their losses were very heavy, ours slight. Here we realized the difference between offensive and defensive warfare. Behind our works we felt secure, and when they came out and charged us three lines deep, we literally mowed them down. Our losses were very slight, our regiment, I think, sustaining the loss of only one man, and he happened to be one of the pickets who were far in our front and who had received the most stringent orders not to be driven in only by a line of battle. The enemy did not try any more to take this road, and we held it to the end of the war.

Our next engagement was Hatcher's Run, which was a disagreeable battle, especially so to your historian, as he happened after the fighting was over to be the division officer of the picket, and was instructed to bring the pickets all off before daylight, the corps having been withdrawn shortly after or about midnight. I recollect I brought the pickets off just at daybreak, and supposed I had them all when I came over the bridge, and I so reported to division headquarters. I was then asked where the 150th Pennsylvania Volunteers were. They had not been heard from since the fight the morning before. This was the first intimation I had that they were over there and had been sent out as skirmishers before the battle. I told the general I would go and try and find them. When I got down to the Run our men had removed the planks and left only the stringers, so I left my horse and told the pickets stationed there where to take him in case I did not return. I thought I had a passport to a Southern prison sure, but it turned out otherwise. I ran into a man who had just left them, and he said they were lost and did not know which way to get out. We hurried to them just as a line of the enemy were coming on to them in their rear, and they had as many of them in their front as they could look after. As soon as they saw me I beckoned to them, and we made a very hasty exit, the enemy closely following us. We had two men wounded before we reached the bridge, but with the aid of the pickets on our side, who opened on them as soon as they saw them, we all came across the stringers of the bridge, not failing to bring along our two wounded comrades.

Our next engagement was Chapin Farm, then Dabney's Mills. In this battle we only had about seventy-five men of our regiment engaged, and there were seven color-bearers of our regiment killed and wounded that afternoon, and I had my horse shot. I think our loss in killed and wounded that afternoon was twenty-one. By this those of you that did not happen to be present may know it was anything but a picnic. After this battle we were soon in winter quarters.

During the winter our corps, with a division of cavalry, made a raid nearly to the border of North Carolina, and destroyed about twenty miles of railroad, and on our return trip burned everything in the country for half a mile wide. This devastation was brought about by reason of our men finding some of their comrades, who had straggled and were probably foraging, hanging to a tree with their throats cut. After this event, orders to guard any kind of property was a useless waste of words ; the men were desperate, and they left a desolation along their path (and it was through a most lovely country) that I doubt not to a large extent exists to-day, after a quarter of a century has nearly elapsed. During the winter the enemy began to desert to our lines more than they had ever done before, and their hard appearance and stories of distress gave us much encouragement that the war would end with the next spring's campaign, which, from preparations going on in our lines, we knew we would be sharp and decisive.

We are about ready to strike, when early one morning, to our surprise, the enemy dashed in and captured the pickets, and obtained possession of Fort Steadman and all the garrison. This fort was situated near the center of our lines round Petersburgh, and the confusion and excitement it caused was, for awhile, very great from one end of our lines to the other. A desperate fight for about two hours ended the affair, however, by our regaining the fort and capturing about 2,500 prisoners. The next night we were packed all up, and at 2 A. M. moved out of camp, left in front again. Whisperings among the knowing ones led us to believe that the task of taking the South Side Railroad, which then was the only source General Lee had of getting supplies, had been allotted to the Fifth Corps and cavalry under Sheridan. Several times during the winter this had been tried, but without success. We knew the march would be short before we struck something to impede our progress. About 8 A. M. an orderly brought me word to drop out of the line with the 142d and 121st and guard the wagon-train, which was passing along our flank and a little to the rear of our column. This, I recollect, pleased us, as it was the first easy duty in time of near action that had ever been given to us, and we all naturally reasoned that the column would find the enemy and have one good battle before our services would be required. About one o'clock our skirmishers commenced business, our train halted, and so did we. Presently, however, an orderly came to me with orders to let the trains take care of themselves, and for us to push up to the front and join the brigade.

This put a new color to our prospects. We, however, obeyed, and almost in no time found our brigade, and went into mass with them just behind a big woods. The skirmishers had evidently found a serious obstacle, for the firing soon became furious, and presently our corps general and his staff came out of the woods flying, and riding up to our brigade commander ordered him into line and to a charge through these woods. This sudden change of things filled the men with enthusiasm, and they went into this charge with more vim and noise than I had ever seen them display before. We passed through the woods, cleared them, and nearly across a large field on the other side, and drove the enemy in flying disorder. So willing were the troops for pursuit that is was difficult to stop them. In order to let the remainder of the corps come up, for the protection of our flanks, soon a volunteer skirmish line was called for, and the whole line moved forward and we were obliged to halt them and make a detail. This accomplished, the lines all up and formed, it commenced raining—no, pouring—and for thirty-six hours it continued to come down in torrents. When it cleared up we pushed forward a short distance over the Boydton plank road, and massed in some thick pines. We hoped here to be able to build fires and dry our clothes and arms before again going into action, but we were soon informed by our skirmishers that the enemy were advancing, and we were taken out of these wood on a double-quick, down a hill and through a stream of water that took the men to their waists; up the hill, forward into line, and we commenced firing. The 142d, as we came up the hill, struck a knoll which seemed to slope every way in our favor. The enemy in our front were pouring in a tremendous shower of bullets; I ordered the men to lie down and commence firing as fast as ever they could, which they did. Their firing being low was very effective, for in our immediate front we were holding them, and giving them more than they wished for. We are not very far from Five Forks and the South Side Road, and I was in great hopes that before night we should have it. We kept the enemy busy in our front, but to our right and left our lines gave away and were falling back. It was so smoky and foggy we could not see the color of the clothing of the troops to our right and left, and we held our front good until ordered by an aid sent to me to fall back with much haste as we were nearly surrounded. The order was given, and down the hill we went, and through the stream before spoken of. Quite a number were captured before we got to the stream; and as my horse landed on the opposite bank, I stopped him and turned for the purpose of taking the colors from our sergeant, thinking I could possibly run the gauntlet and save them better on my horse than he could on foot, for I was fearful lest the whole regiment would be gobbled, the enemy being even and in some places in advance of us on both our flanks. The sergeant—a very brave boy he was—assured me he would bring them out all right; and just as he said it I received a gun-shot wound in the side, which, for a time, took all the breath out of me; and to obviate capture, if possible, I dropped my reins, grabbed the pommel of my saddle, and applied the spurs as vigorously as I could in my fainting condition. The minie-ball that lodged in my side weighed only an ounce, but it felt, as I was going back towards the field, as though it was a twelve-pound cannon-ball.

Our men rallied on the brow of the next hill, where our artillery had wheeled into battery, and sent the enemy back faster than they had advanced "by a large majority." I went to City Point Hospital after having been patched up and bandaged in the field hospital. I had to ride about twenty miles in an ambulance, much of the way over corduroy roads, and in with another poor fellow who had lost his leg; and from my recollection of the journey, when we arrived at its end I was pretty well used up.

The next morning our forces advanced and took the Southside Railroad, Five Forks, and about 13,000 prisoners. This broke the enemy all up, and General Lee immediately thereafter withdrew from Petersburgh and tried hard to make good his escape, which he failed to do, so closely was he pursued by our cavalry and forces of every branch of the service.

Five Forks was the last hard-fought battle of the war. After it, for five or six days, our army pursued with all the vigor of a victorious host, and had some little skirmishes, but no great battles, and at Appomattox Court House the great General of the Army of Northern Virginia found himself so completely hemmed in and surrounded that sooner than see the useless waste of the lives of his brave army he sent to our lines a flag of truce. And soon the news of his surrender was heralded to the world. All lovers of the Union rejoiced, and all our soldiers had such respect for the men they had been fighting so long, that almost in no time after the surrender they were dividing with them their rations and showing them every consideration of kindness in their power.

Returning after my absence on account of my wounds, I met the regiment a short distance from Alexandria, after their long march from Appomattox, my wounds having sufficiently recovered to enable me to join them in time to take part in the last grand review at Washington.

Immediately after this orders to muster out the troops, by reason of the end of the war, were issued by the War Department, and as there was much to do in mustering out a regiment so long in active service, as every man that had ever belonged to the regiment had to be accounted for, and a general settlement with the government had to be made, I was thankful to be able to be with them to direct and help all I could in bringing this about with as little delay as possible, for now that the war was over all were anxious to see home and friends. In the performance of these last duties the regiment and her officers were highly complimented for promptness, as her papers were in readiness, and she was the second regiment mustered out after the order was issued, and the second one to leave Washington for home. As her commander, your historian always felt a little pride over this, and also the fact that when we left Washington he had in his possession a certificate of non-indebtedness from the second auditor of the War Department, which document he has always prized next to his commissions and his honorable discharge.

After mustering out at Washington, we went to Harrisburg, drew our final pay and bade each other farewell, returning to our homes after an absence of three years, lacking a few days, with the sublime satisfaction of having accomplished that for which we had volunteered. And thus, my comrades, ends this history of your old regiment, written in the shortest way possible, necessarily leaving out a great deal that might be of much interest to all, but, which would make the story too voluminous for an occasion like this. Is it any wonder, after an experience of service such as we had, it does us good to meet here and know each other once again, and recall the scenes through which we passed, and the memory of those comrades whose life-blood cemented our glorious Union and made it not only possible, but practicable and true ; that all men were born free and equal, and that a government "of the people, by the people and for the people," if properly and honestly conducted, is a government that will stand the storms of all foreign and internal controversies, and will be blessed and perpetuated by Almighty God for all time to come.

I thank you, comrades, for listening so attentively to this history which you helped to make, and which I know would be much more interesting if better told.

Our losses from the time of our enlistment until our discharge, as taken from the records of the War Department, are as follows: Total enrollment 935 men; killed and died of wounds, 7 officers, 133 men; wounded, 21 officers, 409 men; died of disease, etc., 21 officers, 81 men; captured and missing, 2 officers, 156 men; total loss, 809. This percentage of losses, comrades, I am credibly informed is greater than any regiment that was in the service, with the exception of two. So you can reasonably say that your regiment was eminently a fighting regiment, and her record will bear you out in the assertion. With this last information, comrades, I draw my short history to a close by appending a list of the general engagements in which we participated in order as they came.

List of Battles.

Fredericksburgh,	North Anna River.
Burnside Mud March.	Bethesda Church.
Chancellorsville.	Cold Harbor.
Gettysburg.	Petersburgh.
Frankstown.	Weldon Railroad.
Thoroughfare Gap.	Hatcher's Run.
Rappahannock Station.	Dabney's Mills.
Meade's Retrograde Movement.	Hatcher's Run 2d.
Wilderness.	Fort Steadman.
Laurel Hill.	Boydton Plank Road.
Spottsylvania.	Five Forks.
Tolopotomy Creek.	Appomattox.

The same officers were then re-elected for two years, and it was decided to hold our next reunion at Somerset, Pa., the second Tuesday of September, 1891.

The regiment then marched to the place designated for our monument on Reynolds Avenue and proceeded to dedicate the same, as follows:

Reading of selections from the Scriptures by Comrade Brown, after which the following prayer was offered up by the Rev. Dr. Tomlinson:

PRAYER.

Almighty God, we thank Thee that we have been permitted to meet together on this occasion. We thank Thee that the smiles of Heaven beam upon us with uncommon refulgence; that our circumstances, though solemn and impressive, are altogether different from what they once were, when this spot and the whole country surrounding us were drenched with blood and strewed with the bodies of brave and patriotic heroes. We thank Thee for what Thou hast done for us as individuals and as a nation. We bless Thy name that, when this country was in imminent peril—yea, in the very throes of dissolution—there were brave and loyal men all over this land of freedom who were willing to forsake home and friends, and go into the arena of strife and die to perpetuate our government, and to preserve to us our liberties, civil and religious. We thank Thee that Thou didst give us success and victory over our enemies. We thank Thee especially that we are privileged to meet together for the purpose of consecrating this monument to the memory of our fallen heroes, and of offering them this tribute of honor, of love and esteem. May we ever remember them with gratitude and respect for their devotion to the cause of freedom. May these soldiers who survived and are here to-day, rejoice in Thy favor and resolve to consecrate themselves anew to the love of home and country, and to the cause of Him who loved them and gave Himself for them. May we all, as soldiers and acquaintances met together—as we shall probably never meet again—think of our latter end, and determine to be more faithful in the future than we have been in the past, so that when the conflicts of life are over, we may all meet in Heaven where there will be no strife, no insurrection, no rebellion, no war; but where all will be peace and rest forevermore.

Bless all who may now or hereafter be engaged in similar services on this great battle-field. May all have occasion to rejoice in Thee, the God of their salvation. Hear us, O Lord God, in all these things and answer us graciously, for Christ's sake. Amen!

Colonel Warren then delivered the following address, which was listened to attentively:

Address of Colonel H. N. Warren.

Comrades: We are here to-day to perform one of the most solemn duties of our lives—to dedicate this monument to the sacred memory of our brave and faithful associates, who, a quarter of a century ago, marched with us, shoulder to shoulder, in the line of duty, and who did more than we, for, as Providence would have it, they gave up their lives that their country might live.

This beautiful monument of granite, erected, paid for and presented by the grand old Keystone State, is a fitting and eloquent testimonial of the kindly feelings of love and charity she has always entertained and displayed for her loyal sons. Comrades, it becomes us as survivors of the 142d Pennsylvania Volunteers, this day and upon this public occasion, to thank in our inmost hearts the loyal citizens of this commonwealth, through our distinguished comrade who governs them, for their kindness and liberality in erecting upon this sacred soil this lasting tribute to our old regiment, of whose services we are all justly proud ; and to our fallen comrades, who were, by the casualties of war, transferred from our muster rolls to the muster roll on high.

This monument, comrades, will tell the world—yes, generations yet unborn—that the men who composed the 142d Pennsylvania Volunteers were patriots ; it will be a silent yet potential monitor, proclaiming our sacrifice to Loyalty, our love for the Union and our devotion to the Stars and Stripes. It will impress our children, when we are gone, with the fact that their fathers dared to die that their country might live, and that the blessings of civil liberty might be perpetuated and handed down to them unimpaired ; and, unless I go far astray in my prophesy, it will inspire them with the same spirit of loyalty manifested by this generation, when it gave over half a million of lives to make true and complete the declaration of our forefathers that "*all men are created equal.*"

This monument, comrades, will live for ages after we have gone to rest "under the shade of the trees." It will be an evidence that the 142d Pennsylvania Volunteers was one of the regiments of the old First Corps, which, on the 1st of July, 1863, under the gallant Reynolds, first intercepted and gave battle to the great army of invaders who were then, with almost superhuman efforts, trying to transfer the seat of war into Pennsylvania, lay waste her beautiful homes, and, if possible, capture and take possession of her populous cities, when they could reasonably sue for a peace, such as might be agreeable to themselves. The result we all know, and we of the Union Army who still live cannot but rejoice that the issue terminated as it did, and that to us, in the outcome—

"The lines are fallen in pleasant places, and we have a goodly heritage."

Captain Snowden, late Captain of Company I, then spoke as follows:

ADDRESS OF CAPTAIN GEORGE R. SNOWDEN.

COMRADES OF THE 142D PENNSYLVANIA VOLUNTEERS: We have gathered here to-day from distant parts, even from beyond the borders of the State, to dedicate the monument raised by a grateful commonwealth to commemorate the services of our command. We assemble on this spot, sacred to the memories of our fallen friends, with feelings blended alike with joy and sorrow. It stirs us with joy unspeakable to see again our associates of other days, our companions on the march, in bivouac, and in battle, and to grasp the outstretched hand that nourished us when ill or supported us when wounded, and to renew old recollections and friendships; and with sorrow to observe that "the moving accidents of field and flood" have left so few to tell the tale of great events now long gone by. The eye overflows and the voice can scarcely be trusted to speak the emotions of the heart. While kindly nature has with tree, and brush, and flower, covered gaping rents made in the rude conflict of arms, the lapse of time leaves its indelible marks upon those whom the fortunes of war and of peace have left to survive. In the quarter of a century elapsed since you were mustered out, slender youths have become stalwart men, "bearded like the pard," and those a little older have advanced beyond the line of middle age; upon others the frosts have left their traces, and, alas! others who escaped the perils of battle have gone to join the silent and ever-increasing majority.

It remains for us to renew the story of the regiment, and while we may not recall our absent comrades from their silent abodes, we may pay fit tribute to virtues which led them to noble service in behalf of the cause for which they fell. While they perished in restoring a broken Union, they established the enduring fame of their beloved regiment. Regrets are vain that they lived not to see the day when, as now, the character of the 142d Pennsylvania Volunteers for heroism, devotion, and other martial qualities, is acknowledged to be the highest type of the American Volunteer. Modest, patient, obedient, it did its work for no motives other than those of patriotism and fidelity to duty in whatever shape it might assume, regardless of whatsoever consequences might ensue, knowing only the oath of fidelity to the Government, and the noble impulses of hearts which had rather calmly face death with feet to the foe than ignominiously turn their back.

As much could have been expected and foretold from the character of the men who filled up its ranks, for they represented the diverse pursuits and composite character of the American citizen. Among them were the followers of the learned professions, men in business, bankers, mechanics of all kinds, drillers of oil-wells, miners of coal and iron, farmers, clerks, producers and manufacturers of lumber, teachers—in fact of almost every branch of industry—and generous and spirited boys from school, college, and the shop. The sturdy Pennsylvania Dutch were there, with their simple ways and honest hearts; the stern and resolute Scotch-Irish, the indomitable Welsh, the pertinacious English, the gallant and impetuous Irish, the steadfast Scotch, and the American of every extraction, Protestant and Catholic, all met on the level of citizenship and of patriotism. Made up of such elements the regiment formed a fit type of the State and of the country at large, and consequently in no other organization was the sentiment more prevalent and powerful which led every one to feel that the war was his personal fight. Inspired, then, with the conviction that their individual interests, their future prosperity, their homes, and, above all, the honor, welfare and perpetuity of their country, native and adopted, were at stake, no sacrifice, no hardship, no danger was too great for them patiently to meet and successfully to undergo. With the cheerful spirit of obedience, the bowing of the neck to the voluntary yoke of discipline, was the lofty emotion of rivalry with other regiments, the resolution not to be outdone in feats of valor when tending to useful ends, for they had not the *gaudium certaminis*, the joy of conflict—few in either army felt it—and to hold the reputation of the command not only free from reproach, but clear, bright, luminous with deeds of heroism and endurance.

Officers and men alike entered the army with little or no preparatory training. The number of officers who were instructed in tactics could be counted on the fingers of one hand. As an illustration of the ignorance which prevailed of the simplest details: A lieutenant in temporary command on the first formation of the regiment put the right of his company where the left ought to have rested, and seeing the other troops with their arms at an order—those Belgian rifles of sorrowful memory—to conform to the movement innocently directed his men to "ground arms." But the colonel had been captain of Company A, Tenth Reserves, and the major had seen some experience in the three-months' service. Drilling, however, persistent and intelligent, soon brought the mass of raw recruits to a high state of discipline and efficiency, which enabled them to make an illustrious record and to stand with credit and distinction by the side of older and more experienced organizations.

Aware of its own merits it never sought popular applause, and it was satisfied with the consciousness of duty well done. Sensible to praise and grateful for approval in those quarters where criticism was just and valuable, it was content to rely upon the truth of impartial history for its place in the niche of fame. If, on the one hand, it was seldom that a newspaper writer or any army correspondent mentioned it in the pages of the press, which were too often used for the glorification of favorite leaders and pet regiments, on the other it escaped, for it did not deserve, animadversion or censure. Now, however, that the merits of the various commands are being reviewed and carefully weighed in the public prints by accurate and capable writers, we should be unjust to our departed comrades, to ourselves, and to our children, did we not proudly and confidently assert our claim to a superiority which is being tardily and somewhat reluctantly conceded. Far be it from us in any way to detract from the well-earned reputation of other regiments, our gallant comrades in arms; but it can do them no wrong confidently to assert our right. Nor is it inconsistent with the modesty which sought no especial distinction, but was content to do its full duty unheralded by the blare of trumpets which attended the exploits of our fellows, now that the books are open and the accounts being audited and settled, to ask no more and to accept no less than that which is justly our due.

Of individual and personal gallantry, instances enough might be cited to fill a book; they were common to all grades, from the commanding officer to the private in his blouse. The simple soldier in the ranks rivalled his colonel in exposure to danger, in fervid and romantic devotion to the honor of his flag, in resolute advance upon the enemy, in firm, sullen, yea, defiant retreat before a foe for the moment too strong to be overcome, ready at a favorable moment to turn and restore the fortune of the hour. The men whose first experience of marching was on that memorable October day when they moved from Sharpsburg to South Mountain, in a storm lasting without intermission from one morning until near the dawn of the next, too tired and sleepy to stand about the feeble fires sputtering and sizzling in the rain, too wet to lie down, were the same who, when Lieut-Colonel McCalmont, in his stirring speech before they moved against the heights of Fredericksburgh, regretted the absence from illness of their beloved colonel, and asked them well to do their duty as became citizens of Pennsylvania and soldiers of the republic, responded with ringing cheers, to the amazement of the reserves and perhaps to the wonder of the Confederates whom they were on the way to meet. Later, in the thick of the fight when, risen from a sick-bed at Washington, hastening to the field on hearing that the army had crossed the Rappahannock, Colonel Cummins rode up at a furious gallop and was received with another burst of applause such as must have convinced him, if necessary, of the affection of his regiment for him and of their coolness in time of battle. On that disastrous field, where it first met the enemy and received its baptism of fire, two hundred and fifty of our comrades, one-third of those who went into action, including our gallant Major Bradley, attested by their blood their heroism and devotion to the cause. The sacrifice was in vain, for although the division under Meade broke the hostile lines and threatened to turn their right flank, the only one which accomplished so much, not being supported by other and fresher troops within easy reach, the 142d slowly fell back, with a solid front opposed to the advancing foe.

Passing with credit through the Chancellorsville campaign, where at Pollock's Mills and elsewhere on the left it withstood a severe artillery fire with calmness and fortitude, and afterwards on the extreme right it confronted Stonewall Jackson's veterans, and with the First Corps covered the retreat of the army. On this fateful and bloody field the regiment gained imperishable renown and shed additional lustre upon the country and the flag. The story of the battle cannot be told without alluding to this very spot, where you stood on that disastrous first day of July and unflinchingly faced an adversary flushed with recent victories and greater in strength and position. How well you performed your part cannot be known alone from dreary records which in figures coldly speak of losses, but history as yet unwritten when fully unfolded will reveal to your admiring countrymen a contest against largely superior forces which will reflect glory upon your name as long as the Union and civilization shall last, longer far than this stone shall stand unbroken before the elements.

Pushed by the necessity of reaching the ground at an early hour, wearied by a forced march from Marsh Creek, you promptly formed line and opened fire. Only when Reynolds had fallen and you were outflanked were you pushed back. Your brigade commander grasped your colors and led you to a hopeless charge, an act of personal gallantry undoubtedly, but unwise, rash, leading to misfortune which might not otherwise have occurred. Your colonel, the heroic Cummins, borne off in faithful arms, gave up his noble life as a seal to his devotion. Forming a barricade in front of yonder Seminary you still faced outward and only when again outflanked did you slowly retire under McCalmont, flag in hand, through the town, fighting, resolute, defiant. Like Cæsar's legion, you put all hope of safety only in your own bravery. On reaching the Cemetery, preserving your organization, observing the long lines of hostile infantry encircling your position, you held it until relieved by reinforcements of fresh troops. On the 2d and 3d you firmly kept the dangerous and responsible places assigned to you, and, while not again exposed to great loss, you well performed your duty and supported your comrades, who were more actively and fortunately engaged in winning the final victory which hurled back the invader, never more to lift his head north of the Potomac.

To this brief and imperfect review of your conduct on the field must be added figures taken from yonder inscription, which has been verified by the official records. Out of a total of 336 officers and men, 125 only escaped casualty, and 211 fell in action, were wounded or carried into captivity—a loss of 63 per centum—greater, I am confident, than that sustained by any other regiment, however much it may have suffered, or however conspicuous it was in these sanguinary conflicts. Many other men equally brave died with the lion-like Cummins, and others, as one may see about him, offered up their limbs, glowing with youth and strength, sacrifices upon the common altar of patriotism. Well may a writer, to this day unknown, in the editorial columns of the Philadelphia *Ledger*, on the 11th day of July, 1863, remark: " Few regiments in any circumstances or service could show a nobler record than this. All honor to the memory of these brave men, who left all their hopes and prospects of life, not for fame, but from a sense of duty to their State, their country, and not these alone, but to the free institutions and principles therein represented, principles in which are bound up the noblest feelings and dearest interests of humanity.

From this place, in rapid pursuit of the Confederates, the regiment returned to the Rappahannock, swiftly withdrew to Bull Run and Centreville, arriving at the latter point by forced marches, one of which was from Kelly's Ford to Bristow—a distance of thirty-one miles—in time to seize the heights before the enemy's cavalry could occupy them. Going back to the Rapidan it passed the winter in quarters at Culpepper. In the spring of 1864, on the reorganization of the army under General Grant, and the disruption of the old renowned First Corps—a matter of lasting and profound regret to all who had served with it—the 142d became part of the Third Brigade, First Division, General Wadsworth, and Fifth Corps, General Warren. Time will not suffice, and the approaching storm will not permit, to name and describe the battles, movements and sieges in which it afterward engaged, for to do so would be to recapitulate the history of Grant's campaigns in Virginia. It is enough to say that in the closing scenes of Five Forks and Appomattox, it was ever in the advance and wound up an eventful and memorable career in a blaze of glory. Through your ranks went the flag of truce which led to the surrender, and Grant rode to the final meeting with Lee. You received your late foes with open arms and, as generous and considerate as you were brave in the last irretrievable victory, you divided with them the contents of your haversacks. Thence by marches easy to you, but severe to others of less training, you came to Washington, where, after the grand review on which the eyes of the world were fixed with attention and astonishment, the Army of the Potomac ceased to exist, living only in the pages of history, and the hearts of the survivors and of a grateful country. At Harrisburg the fragment of veterans, weary with service, bronzed by the weather, and battered by wounds, was mustered out, and they returned to mingle with their fellow-citizens, conscious of a great duty well done, and content that their achievements should speak for themselves. Later investigation has well justified that confidence. Able and accurate writers have shown that of all the organizations on either side, one only, a short-term regiment from North Carolina, met with casualties so numerous in proportion, and only one other, the 141st Pennsylvania, can claim right to compare with the 142d in the extent of its sacrifice to preserve the Union.

Few commands saw so much hard service, none suffered greater proportionate loss. Of an aggregate of 935, all told, 809 met with the accidents of war, in death, wounds, disease, and other ways incident to protracted campaigns, and only 126 responded to roll-call for the last time. The history of the regiment remains to be written. Deeds of heroism and endurance, such as it performed, at times even unconscious to itself of their brilliancy or value, ought not to be left to the oblivion of musty records, or merged in the achievements of large bodies. A fruitful field is open to some writer gifted with an accurate and judicious pen and patient research, and moved by admiration for heroism seldom if ever surpassed since the world rolled out from the hands of its Creator.

But, my comrades, little remains now to be said. We shall soon disperse to our homes and many of us will never again meet on earth. As you go your several ways, however, you are conscious that while long deferred and eagerly contested, the impartial verdict has now been rendered and your claims to superiority for bravery and devotion not only are not denied, but are freely conceded by persons most familiar with events which took place in the course of the great rebellion.

As the shades of evening slowly settle down upon you and age withers stalwart frames which here and elsewhere did glorious battle for liberty, it will be a proud consolation to recall your unequalled services and to remember that you fought under a regimental flag which, while it knew defeat and victory, never knew dishonor. You have the satisfaction, after all your toil, danger and hardship, of knowing that the fame of the regiment is constantly becoming more conspicuous and illustrious, and that when all the truth shall finally be generally settled and acknowleged, the topmost tablet of the history of the war will record in indelible characters the achievements of the 142d Pennsylvania Volunteers.

The following touching address was then listened to:

ADDRESS OF PRIVATE JAMES E. MACLANE.

MY DEAR COMRADES AND FRIENDS: After listening to those preceding me, I feel that I cannot add anything new or that would be interesting. As one of Company "I," I wish to express my love and esteem for my comrades; and am proud to say that I was a member of this regiment. This is a most pleasing scene, and yet, what pangs and peculiar sensations pass through our minds as we take a retrospective view! Think of the missing comrades, and of our experiences of twenty-seven years ago, as they pass before us in panoramic view.

At that time most all of us were boys, not many having arrived at the age of twenty-one years. This is particularly so in my case. I was associated with you in but one campaign, but that was a very active one. As a participant and an observer at that time, it was forced upon my mind that our regiment was one of the best for any service required. It was not associated with that influence during the war that manufactured "brilliant officers" in large head-lines in our newspapers at home, nor was it assigned to a brigade that had any particular reputation for fighting or that was conspicuous, until its connection with the Pennsylvania Reserves in 1862 and 1863. This experience formed part of our early military education and training. We soon became veterans and knew how to replace a missing gun or blanket, or do things necessary to establish a reputation as soldiers in that line. At this point let me ask you to go back to those days. Can you see our wagon covers, with the large letters and figures displayed, *142d Regiment, P. R. V. C.*, thus recruiting and apparently adding one hundred more regiments to that famous old division? What scrutiny and feeling that inscription engendered! But by the more intimate association with the 3d, 4th, 7th and 8th Regiments of the Reserves, this was soon changed, as, by relationship, our colonel came from the 10th Regiment of the original organization.

Your first trial and baptism was a convincing proof of your ability to stand. That I have from the highest authority, from those living and some that have passed away. No regiment stood up any better under a severe fire, and with less confusion in falling back, than you did. I have heard the common saying, which is an old one, "*You knew no better;*" but you did know better, and circumstances that stimulated you at the time prove it.

The old division officers and men of the Reserves all seem to have the warmest affection and respect for our regiment, and are solicitous that we should complete our roll of the survivors of the 142d Regiment, to be registered, and have their addresses placed in the hands of the secretary, Captain John Taylor, at Philadelphia, for membership in that association.

After my being disabled and sent away north to a hospital, finding my injuries and disease permanent, I could not but follow you in my mind, with pride at your soldierly conduct; and yet with sorrow in my heart when I thought of all your marches and engagements. I thought of the killed and wounded, wondering to myself : Can I ever see them again ? can I see our regimental flag with battles inscribed on every stripe as I saw others ? will our regiment gain that renown ? In this mood a jealous feeling of sympathy often caused me to think that my mind was wandering. I would be prompted as if by a spirit from you, saying, " Who composed the regiment ?" The significant and imaginary answer would awaken every thought, and a happy yet sad realization. You were making your own history. I feel indebted to you, particularly to those that went through to the end ; and shall always honor you and point with pleasure to the fact that the composition of our regiment, both in officers and men, was such that has compelled history to place it among the highest when inscribing the " niches " of honor.

To you, comrades of Company " I," my boyhood companions, many of you, I desire to speak a few words. I would not detract from any company of the regiment anything that goes to make up its full meed of praise, and I know the regiment will allow me to address you as an individual company—an opportunity I never expect to have again. Our composition was a varied element, recruited from the hills and valleys of old Venango County. Among us was some of the best blood of the sturdy pioneer, and from the oldest families of refinement and education. I could dwell upon names, but my sympathies and tender feelings for those missing will not allow me at this time. Those from the Oil City district, mostly young mechanics, were my immediate associates. Our political complexion was noted at that time, but soon vanished. All differences in that line were obliterated in the determination of fighting for the defense of one principle that would make us a united and happy people ; a principle that would in the end shine forth as a great halo, reflecting its rays over the peaceful valleys, gilding the old hills of our youth, and leaving to us in our memories the motto of our regiment, " *The love of country guides us.*"

Upon this solemn occasion, as we are dedicating this monument to the memory of our organization, who would not, in silent meditation, pause and drop a tear of affection while thinking of Colonel Cummins? On this hallowed spot of ground, and upon this occasion, a review of his character as a man and a soldier, at my hands, is not required, as it has already been so eloquently and affectionately portrayed by Colonel Warren, Captain Snowden, and others.

I shall never forget my first trial as to valor. The stock that makes the soldier, that sets the example and encourages others, was not in me. On the left, below and opposite Fredericksburgh, Va., May, 1863, we were under a very heavy artillery fire; the regiment protected itself as best it could in a ravine, lying down, and some taking refuge in a ditch. Colonel Cummins hailed me and wished a canteen of water in exchange for a canteen of "*Elixir*," which I most readily consented to. I held the horse while he rearranged his baggage and canteens on his saddle. While in the act of passing the canteen to him after receiving the "Elixir," in apparently less time than could be counted, about half a dozen shells and shot passed in close proximity to his head, and the colonel was only saved by turning in his saddle that moment to give the command, "Fall in!" The check or curb-rein was twisted, and I was in the act of straightening it out when a shot struck the horse below the eye and carried the lower part of the head away. I had the rein and bit on my arm and shoulder; I was horror-stricken and fell to the ground, as something struck me in the head, back of the left ear. In an instant I was up again and surely thought the shell or shot went through the body of the colonel, but was startled and surprised to see him, with apparent coolness, getting off the horse as the latter was slowly sinking upon his haunches, the colonel urging me with some emphasis to get "traps" off the saddle. This apparent coolness on his part was, to a certain extent, a stimulant to my nerves. I conceitedly supposed at the time I was really a veteran, and my lesson from him served to support me in many after-contingencies. This incident is upon record as one of the cases of singular vitality, related of wounded battery, cavalry and infantry horses. Imagine a horse with the major part of his head shot away, and running over the field! Some comrade—I think Sergeant Wood of Company "A"—and myself fired several shots from revolvers into his head and neck, but the horse seemed invincible, as the shots did not kill him. Colonel Joseph K. Davison, late of the 29th New Jersey Volunteers, has told me since that the horse was running around after we had marched off to the right. So, doubtless, you could all relate many incidents of the war, and I will pass with referring to just one more. When presenting the black horse to Colonel Cummins, at White Oak Church, Va., do you recollect his remarks in accepting the gift?

"I can cut or maul rails, I can saw wood, I can farm or grub, I can work at anything, but *I can't make a speech.*" The simplicity and honesty of his statement, and the expression of his countenance while expressing it, forced upon my mind the fact that we had no coward for a commander, but one that would fight, and see that others did so, if occasion required.

The award of the contract of the design of the monument selected by the regimental committee, was, I am sorry to say, refused acceptance by the State Board of Commissioners. This, at the time, was a severe blow to our committee, to myself and to others. Subsequent events, however, have demonstrated that the commissioners endeavored to do what was best in the matter, and as a regiment we owe a great deal to the comrades and gentlemen composing it for the interest they have manifested in the erection of this monument. This is especially true of the secretary of the Board, Colonel John P. Nicholson, who was untiring in his efforts in our behalf, and is entitled to the thanks of every member of the regiment.

Now, comrades, thanking you kindly for your attention, and believing my feelings and expressions to be the sentiment of one common family, I bid you an affectionate good-by.

After which Lieutenant Miller spoke the following words:

Address of Lieutenant John V. Miller.

Comrades: We, the survivors of the 142d Regiment of Pennsylvania Volunteers, after the lapse of over a quarter of a century, have been permitted to assemble on this field of Gettysburg, where so many of our comrades went down in battle. They did not live to enjoy the thrill of joy that victory gives to those that contend in battle here. On this field the light of their lives went out amid the roar of cannon and the rattle of musketry—some of them in the throes of agony, while conscious that our little force was being overpowered, before death came to their relief. At the mention of the name of our brave and gallant commander, Colonel Cummins, every eye will turn to the spot where he fell helplessly wounded, and yet with sufficient life in him to know that the day was lost. Picture, if you can, his thoughts and feelings for the few moments that he lived, as he saw his brave regiment repulsed and forced from the field by the advancing thousands of Lee's army! But death soon came to his relief, and shut out from his eyes forever the brave boys of his regiment, for whom he had given his best thought and most watchful care on the march, in camp, and on the battle-field.

My thoughts this day are drawn in an especial manner toward yonder grove in front of the Seminary. It was there that Lieutenant Tucker, our acting adjutant, fell, after having been wounded twice previously to receiving his fatal wound—a young man, scarcely twenty-one, bright in intellect, a genial companion and a whole-souled soldier.

After the lapse of all these years, our thoughts go back to our young comrades, and we sometimes feel that it was indeed hard for the young soldier just stepping on the threshold of life, his heart throbbing and his spirits bounding to the impulse of hope in the coming years, to take his young life to the field, and in one short rush end it. They were all young men, and every foot of ground from this spot to the Seminary was pressed by their feet as they contended with the overpowering force of the enemy; and many a young and ardent soldier was stricken down from our regiment on this plain, who will never answer to his name this side of that Grand Army that is constantly going up to swell its ranks in the great Beyond.

My comrades, I greet you to-day. It is fitting that we meet on this field where so many of our comrades have attested their valor and gave their lives a willing sacrifice to their country and flag. This monument we dedicate to the heroes of our regiment who fell at Gettysburg. All honor to them! It will tell to all people in all time of the patriotism and valor of the men of the 142d Pennsylvania Volunteers, not only at Gettysburg but in all the battles and marches from Fredericksburgh to Appomattox.

Let our comradeship that was welded in the fire of so many battles, fashioned by the long marches that tested our endurance, and sealed by the large number of our dead on many fields of glory, continue until the last man has been mustered out and we have joined the regiment again on the other shore.

Private Horner, late of Company C, addressed the veterans substantially as follows:

Address of Private D. J. Horner.

Comrades of the 142d Regiment, Pennsylvania Volunteers: I am glad to be with you to-day and join in dedicating this monument to the memory of the gallant men of the 142d Regiment who on this historic field helped to uphold the flag of our common country, and by their gallantry and bravery, in common with all the Union forces, drove back the invading hosts of Lee, and by the splendid victory they achieved in the field virtually destroyed the power of the enemy and rendered the final victory certain.

It was not within my province to be with you on that memorable occasion, as I was then completely disabled, having been severely wounded in the battle of Fredericksburgh, in which one of my limbs was donated to the cause of our country. Standing here and looking over this far-famed battle-field, a feeling of sadness comes into my heart when I think of how many of our brave comrades fell here, and notably our gallant Colonel R. P. Cummins, who was among the first to lead forth the "Frosty Sons of Thunder" from old Somerset County to battle for the Constitution and the Union. But after the lapse of so many years, and after the splendid results of our civil war, there is mingled with this feeling of sadness that of delight at the thought that they did not die in vain; that their blood was shed in a righteous cause, and that out of the sacrifice so nobly made by them our country has been saved, its institutions preserved and the domain of human freedom enlarged. So that the day may be not far distant when the people of other nations will enjoy the same liberty we possess. May this monument erected to-day stand through all the ages, and bear testimony to the bravery and devotion of our noble comrades of the 142d Regiment of Pennsylvania Volunteers.

The exercises closed by singing "My Country 't is of Thee," led by Comrade Brown of Company H. Benediction by the Rev. Dr. Tomlinson.

Adjourned.

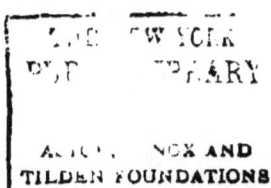

[Inscription on Monument.]

142d Pennsylvania Infantry

1st Brigade, 3d Division, 1st Corps.

Mustered in, August, 1862.
Mustered out, May, 29, 1865.

Recruited in Mercer, Westmoreland, Somerset, Union, Monroe, Pike, Fayette, Venango and Luzerne Counties.

Present at Gettysburg, 336 Officers and Men.
Killed and Died of Wounds, 4 Officers and 27 Men.
Wounded, 10 Officers and 100 Men.
Captured or Missing, 2 Officers and 68 Men.
Total Loss, 211.

Total Enrollment, 935.
Killed and Died of Wounds, 7 Officers and 133 Men.
Wounded, 21 Officers and 409 Men.
Died of Disease, etc., 81 Men.
Captured and Missing, 2 Officers and 156 Men.
Total Loss, 809.

Fredericksburgh, Chancellorsville, Gettysburg, Wilderness, Spottsylvania, North Anna, Tolopotomy, Bethesda Church, Cold Harbor, Petersburgh, Weldon Railroad, Poplar Springs Church, Hatcher's Run, Dabney's Mills, Boydton Road, Five Forks, Appomattox.

July 1, 1863, A. M.—Marched from near Emmettsburg, reaching the field via Willoughby Run. Formed line, facing northward. Occupied this position. Changed it to support artillery. Reformed here and engaged a brigade composed of the 11th, 26th, 47th and 52d North Carolina Infantry. In the afternoon outflanked, and retired, firing, to a position near the Seminary. Here engaged a brigade composed of the 1st, 12th, 13th and 14th South Carolina Infantry. After a gallant fight, again outflanked, and retired to Cemetery Hill.

July 2.—In position at Cemetery Hill.

July 3.—Moved half-mile to the left, and exposed to the artillery fire of the enemy.

COMPLETE ROSTER

OF THE

142d Regiment, Pa. Vols.

1st Brigade, 3d Division, 1st Corps.

ROSTER OF THE REGIMENT.

FIELD AND STAFF OFFICERS.

Name.	Rank.	Mustered into Service.	Remarks.
Robert P. Cummins..	Colonel	Sept. 1, '62,	Died July 2, of wounds received at Gettysburg, Pa., July 1, 1863.
Alfred B. M'Calmont	Lt. Col.	Sept. 1, '62,	Com. Col., July 4, 1863—not mustered—promoted to Col. 208th reg. P. V., Sept., 12, 1864.
Horatio N. Warren..	...do...	Aug. 23, '62,	Pr. fr. Capt. Co. A, to Major, Feb. 2, '64—to Lt. Col., Sept. 17, '64—com. Col—not mus—wd. at Five Forks, Va., April 1, 1865—mus. out with reg., May 20, 1865.
John Bradley	Major...	Sept. 1, '62,	Died Jan. 3, 1863, of wounds received at Fredericksburg, Va., Dec. 13, 1862.
William L. Wilson...	Adjutant	Sept. 1, '62,	Discharged on Surgeon's certificate, Dec. 12, 1863.
Charles P. Orvis.....	..do...	Aug. 31, '62,	Promoted from First Lieut. Co. G., Dec. 19, 1863—discharged Dec. 10, 1864.
H. Warren Stimson..	....do...	Sept. 1, '62,	Promoted from private Co. A, Dec. 30, 1864—mustered out with regiment, May 29, 1865.
William C. Hillman..	Q. M....	Aug. 23, '62,	Mustered out with regiment, May 20, 1865.
Thomas J. Keely.....	Surgeon	Aug. 4, '62,	Pr. from Asst. Surg. 114th reg. P. V., Feb. 12, 1863—mustered out with regiment, May 20, 1865.
Richard C. Halsey...	As. Sur.	Aug. 4, '62,	Discharged March 20, 1863.
J. Lambert Asay.....	..do...	Dec. 27, '62,	Pr. to Surgeon 208th reg. P. V., Sept. 30, 1864.
Chas. E. Humphrey..	...do...	May 28, '63,	Pr. to Surgeon 143d reg. P. V., March 22, 1865.
Abraham M. Barr....	...do...	Mar. 17, '65,	Com. Surgeon—not mustered—mustered out with regiment, May 20, 1865.
William P. Moore....	Chap...	Oct. 25, '62,	Discharged on Surgeon's certificate, Jan. 25, 1865.
William Shields.....	Sr. Maj.	Aug. 28, '62,	Pr. from private Co. E, Mar. 1, '64—wd. at Dabney's Mills, Va., Feb. 6, '65—disch. by G. O., June 24, '65.
Samuel H. Dull	....do...	Aug. 27, '62,	Promoted from Sergt. Co. H—date unknown—transferred to Vet. Res. Corps, Aug. 1, 1863.
Thomas J. Wood...	....do...	Aug. 22, '62,	Pr. fr. 1st Sgt. Co. A, Sept. 1, '63—to 1st Lt., 30th reg. U. S. C. T., February 24, 1864—died Nov. 1, 1864, of wounds received at Petersburg, Va.
John B. Frowald.....	Q. M. Sr.	Sept. 1, '62,	Mustered out with regiment, May 20, 1865.
George L. Dunmire..	Com. Sr.	Aug. 22, '62,	Promoted from private Co. A, Sept. 1, 1862—mustered out with regiment, May 20, 1865.
Joseph E. Mason.....	Hos. St.	Aug. 25, '62,	Promoted from private Co. F, May 1, 1863—mustered out with regiment, May 20, 1865.
Nathan S. Burnett...	...do...	Sept. 1, '62,	Discharged on Surgeon's certificate, March 16, 1863.
William P. Clark.....	Pl. Muc.	Aug. 28, '62,	Promoted from Musician Co. B, March 1, 1864—mustered out with regiment, May 20, 1865.
Joseph Moore.........	...do...	Aug. 27, '62,	Transferred to Co. K, 136th reg. P. V., April 30, 1863.
William J. Reed......	...do...	Aug. 22, '62,	Promoted from Musician Co. A, Sept. 1, 1862—tr. to Vet. Res. Corps—date unknown.

COMPANY A.

Horatio N. Warren..	Captain.	Aug. 23, '62,	Promoted to Major, Feb. 2, 1864.
Frank M. Powell	...do...	Aug. 23, '62,	Pr. from 2d to 1st Lt., Nov. 20, 1862—to Capt., Mar. 1, 1864—wd. at Gettysburg, Pa., July 1, '63, at Wilderness, Va., May 5, 1864, and at Five Forks, April 1, 1865—discharged by special order, June 3, 1865.
Martin A. Gibson....	1st Lieut	Aug. 22, '62,	Pr. fr. Sgt. to 2d Lt., May 19, 1863—to 1st Lt., March 1, 1864—commissioned Captain—not mustered—mustered out with company, May 20, 1865.
Cyrus B. Thompson..	1st Sergt	Aug. 22, '62,	Pr. fr. 1st Sgt., Sept. 1, 1863 wd. at Petersburg, Va., July 14, 1864 commissioned 1st Lt—not mustered—mustered out with company May 29, 1865.
Thomas J. Wood.....	... do ...	Aug. 22, '62,	Promoted to Sergeant Major, Sept 1, 1863.

ONE HUNDRED AND FORTY-SECOND REGIMENT.

Name.	Rank.	Mustered into Service.	Remarks.
Alfred H. Goble	Sergeant	Aug. 22, '62,	Prisoner from July 1, 1863, to June 6, 1864—commissioned 2d Lieut.—not mustered—mustered out with company, May 29, 1865.
Alexander S. Love	do	Aug. 22, '62,	Pr. to Sgt., July 1, '64—mus. out with Co., May 20, '65.
John Harsh	do	Feb. 4, '64,	Promoted to Sergeant, May 1, 1865—tr. to Company G, 50th regiment P. V.—date unknown.
John M'Connell	do	Aug. 22, '62,	Killed at Spottsylvania C. H., Va., May 10, 1864—buried in Burial Grounds Wilderness.
William G. Drum	do	Aug. 22, '62,	Captured at Gettysburg, Pa., July 1, 1863—died at Philadelphia, Mar. 24, 1864—burial rec. April 4, 1864.
Morgan B Shirk	do	Aug. 22, '62,	Captured—died at Florence, S. C., Sept. 30, 1864—burial record, died Sept. 11, 1864, at Andersonville, Georgia grave 8484.
Beriah Orr	Corporal	Aug. 22, '62,	Wounded at Wilderness, Va., May 5, 1864 transferred to Company F, 6th regiment V. R. C.—discharged by General Order, July 10, 1865.
John Gundy, Jr	do	Aug. 22, '62,	Captured at Petersburg, Va., Mar. 31, '65—discharged by General Order, June 3, 1865.
John Hosack	do	Aug. 22, '62,	Wounded at Wilderness, Va., May 5, 1864—absent, in hospital, at muster out.
William Healey	do	Aug. 22, '62,	Mustered out with company, May 29, 1865.
Lester Moore	do	Aug. 22, '62,	Mustered out with company, May 29, 1865.
Edwin F. Stiles	do	Aug. 22, '62,	Discharged March 17, 1863, for wounds received at Fredericksburg, Va., Dec. 13, 1862.
Joseph Jones	do	Aug. 22, '62,	Killed at Gettysburg, Pa., July 1, 1863—buried in National Cemetery, section B, grave 62.
William Jeremiah	do	Aug. 22, '62,	Deserted July 17, 1863.
Robert E. Gundy	Musici'n	Aug. 22, '62,	Mustered out with company, May 29, 1865.
William J. Reed	do	Aug. 22, '62,	Promoted to Principal Musician, Sept. 1, 1862.
Brandon, Thomas	Private	Aug. 22, '62,	Wounded at Fredericksburg, Va., Dec. 13, 1862—mustered out with company, May 29, 1865.
Blair, Joseph S.	do	Aug. 22, '62,	Mustered out with company, May 29, 1865.
Brandon, Wm. C.	do	Aug. 22, '62,	Killed at Fredericksburg, Va., Dec. 13, 1862.
Barnes, George B.	do	Aug. 22, '62,	Died Dec. 15, of wounds received at Fredericksburg, Va., Dec. 13, 1862.
Beaty, William	do	Aug. 22, '62,	Died April 9, 1863.
Brown, Thomas	do	Aug. 22, '62,	Deserted July 20, 1863.
Campman, David	do	Aug. 22, '62,	Mustered out with company, May 29, 1865.
Crossman, Cyrus	do	Aug. 22, '62,	Mustered out with company, May 29, 1865.
Campman, Henry	do	Aug. 22, '62,	Mustered out with company, May 29, 1865.
Corey, John	do	Aug. 22, '62,	Discharged February 21, 1863, for wounds received at Fredericksburg, Va., Dec. 13, 1862.
Coyl, John	do	Aug. 22, '62,	Discharged on Surgeon's certificate, May 13, 1864.
Coleman, John W	do	Aug. 22, '62,	Discharged Sept. 21, for wounds received at Wilderness, Va., May 5, 1864.
Campbell, Samuel D.	do	Aug. 22, '62,	Died Aug. 8, of wounds received at Gettysburg, Pa., July 1, 1863—buried in Nat. Cem., sec. D, grave 59.
Dougherty, H. H.	do	Aug. 22, '62,	Discharged on Surgeon's certificate, Dec. 31, 1862.
Davis, John	do	Aug. 22, '62,	Transferred to Vet. Res. Corps date unknown.
Davis, David	do	Aug. 22, '62,	Transferred to Veteran Reserve Corps, Feb. 15, 1864.
Dunmire, Geo. T.	do	Aug. 22, '62,	Promoted to Commissary Sergeant, Sept. 1, 1862.
Davis, Thomas W.	do	Aug. 22, '62,	Deserted February 15, 1863.
Evans, Lotwig	do	Aug. 22, '62,	Wounded at Gettysburg, Pa., July 1, 1863—discharged by General Order, May 25, 1865.
Ellis, Charles L	do	Aug. 22, '62,	Prisoner from May 5, 1864, to May 16, 1865—mustered out with company, May 20, 1865.
Ediburn, Henry B.	do	Aug. 22, '62,	Transferred to Vet. Res. Corps—date unknown.
Evans, Henry	do	Aug. 22, '62,	Transferred to Vet. Res. Corps—date unknown.
Ewart, John A.	do	Aug. 22, '62,	Tr. to 160th company, 2d battalion, V. R. C.—date unknown—discharged by General Order, July 3, 1865.
Edgar, Joseph A	do	Aug. 22, '62,	Killed at North Anna River, Va., May 23, 1864.
Early, William	do	Aug. 22, '62,	Deserted October 22, 1862.
Ginger, John C	do	Aug. 22, '62,	Mustered out with company, May 29, 1865.
Green, John H.	do	Aug. 22, '62,	Discharged on Surgeon's certificate, Mar. 21, 1864.
Greggs, David	do	Aug. 22, '62,	Captured died at Florence, S. C., August 14, 1864—burial record, died at Andersonville, Ga., August 15, 1864—grave 5735.
Hardman, George H.	do	Aug. 22, '62,	Mustered out with company, May 29, 1865.
Hall, William B.	do	Aug. 22, '62,	Discharged on Surgeon's certificate, March 18, 1865.
Hunt, George	do	Aug. 22, '62,	Died at Smoketown, Md., Oct. 25, 1862—burial record, Nov. 2, 1862 buried in Nat'l Cemetery, Antietam, sec. 26, lot C, grave 229.
Jones, Thomas	do	Aug. 22, '62,	Deserted July 28, 1863.
Jeremiah, John	do	Aug. 22, '62,	Deserted February 15, 1863.

ONE HUNDRED AND FORTY-SECOND REGIMENT.

Name.	Rank.	Mustered into Service.	Remarks.
Koonce, William	Private	Aug. 22, '62,	Discharged on Surgeon's certificate, March 16, 1863.
Lytle, John W.	do	Aug. 22, '62,	Mustered out with company, May 29, 1865.
Leek, William	do	Aug. 22, '62,	Killed February 21, 1863.
Lightner, Wm. L.	do	Aug. 22, '62,	Killed at Wilderness, Va., May 6, 1864.
Marsteller, Lemuel	do	Aug. 22, '62,	Mustered out with company, May 29, 1865.
Morton, James	do	Aug. 22, '62,	Discharged by General Order, May 26, 1865.
Morford, Abijah	do	Aug. 22, '62,	Transferred to Vet. Reserve Corps—date unknown
Morris, James K. P.	do	Aug. 22, '62,	Died June 24, of wounds rec. at Petersburg, Va., June 18, 1864—buried in National Cemetery, Arlington.
M'Cullough, Isaac	do	Aug. 22, '62,	Mustered out with company, May 29, 1865.
M'Nabb, Alexander C	do	Aug. 22, '62,	Discharged on Surgeon's certificate, May 18, 1865.
M'Coy, Alexander	do	Aug. 22, '62,	Transferred to U. S. Navy, April 17, 1864.
Orr, John S.	do	Aug. 22, '62,	Mustered out with company, May 20, 1865.
Orr, William A	do	Aug. 22, '62,	Discharged March 16, 1863, for wounds received at Fredericksburg, Va., Dec. 13, 1862.
Piper, Freeman N.	do	Aug. 22, '62,	Mustered out with company, May 29, 1865.
Patton, Allen C.	do	Aug. 22, '62,	Mustered out with company, May 29, 1865.
Preston, John H.	do	Aug. 22, '62,	Discharged on Surgeon's certificate, July 1, 1863.
Perry, Henry W.	do	Aug. 22, '62,	Discharged on Surgeon's certificate, Feb. 15, 1863.
Rice, Albert	do	Aug. 22, '62,	Mustered out with company, May 29, 1865.
Russell, James H.	do	Aug. 22, '62,	Captured—died at Florence, S. C., July 15, 1865.
Smith, William W.	do	Aug. 22, '62,	Mustered out with company, May 29, 1865.
Smith, John R.	do	Aug. 22, '62,	Mustered out with company, May 29, 1865.
Smith, John	do	Aug. 22, '62,	Discharged on Surgeon's certificate, Mar. 12, 1863.
Stimson, H. Warren	do	Sept. 1, '62,	Promoted to Adjutant, December 30, 1864.
Stewart, Linus M.	do	Aug. 22, '62,	Died Jan. 16, 1863, of wounds received at Fredericksburg, Va., December 13, 1862.
Thompson, Noah M.	do	Aug. 22, '62,	Discharged on Surgeon's certificate, June 29, 1863.
Tate, Alfred	do	Aug. 22, '62,	Captured at Gettysburg, Pa., July 1, 1863—died at Annapolis, Md., Sept. 30, 1863.
Webster, John M.	do	Aug. 22, '62,	Mustered out with company, May 29, 1865.
Williams, William J.	do	Aug. 22, '62,	Mustered out with company, May 29, 1865.
Williams, William T.	do	Aug. 22, '62,	Mustered out with company, May 29, 1865.
Webster, James W.	do	Aug. 22, '62,	Mustered out with company, May 29, 1865.
Williamson, Jas. A.	do	Aug. 22, '62,	Discharged on Surgeon's certificate, Mar. 27, 1863.
Williams, Job	do	Aug. 22, '62,	Discharged on Surgeon's certificate, Aug. 4, 1863.

COMPANY B.

Name.	Rank.	Mustered into Service.	Remarks.
John G. Andrews	Captain	Aug. 27, '62,	Discharged Aug. 20, 1864.
Daniel S. Wilkins	do	Aug. 27, '62,	Pr. from 2d to 1st Lt., July 1, 1864 to Capt., Sept. 21, 1864 mustered out with company, May 29, 1865.
Edward B. Hurst	1st Lt.	Aug. 27, '62,	Killed at Gettysburg, Pa., July 1, 1863.
Daniel S. Tinsman	do	Aug. 26, '62,	Pr. fr. Sgt., Oct. 24, '64 - mus. out with Co. May 29, '65.
Urbannas Hubbs	1st Sgt	Aug. 26, '62,	Pr. from private to Sergt., March 1, 1864—to 1st Sergt. Nov. 1, 1864 - com. 2d Lt. June 3, 1865 - not mustered—discharged by General Order, June 7, 1865.
Albert A. Hasson	do	Aug. 26, '62,	Transferred to 166th Co., 2d batt., Vet. Reserve Corps, Feb. 15, 1864 - discharged by G. O., July 3, 1865.
John M. Kough	Sergeant	Aug. 26, '62,	Mustered out with company, May 29, 1865.
George A. Bare	do	Aug. 28, '62,	Pr. fr. Cor. Nov. 1, '64—mus. out with Co. May 29, '65.
David Wilkins	do	Aug. 28, '62,	Pr. fr. Cor. Nov. 1, '64 mus. out with Co. May 29, '65.
Samuel A. Bare	do	Aug. 26, '62,	Pr. fr. Cor. Nov. 1, '64 - mus. out with Co. May 29, '65.
Thomas Lonergan	do	Aug. 26, '62,	Wounded at Fredericksburg, Va., Dec. 13, 1862—discharged by General Order, March 1, 1864.
Griffith P. Clark	do	Aug. 26, '62,	Tr. to Co. G, 18th reg. Vet. Reserve Corps, Feb. 15, 1864—discharged by General Order, June 29, 1865.
John S. Hood	Corporal	Aug. 26, '62,	Mustered out with company, May 29, 1865.
Samuel Dice	do	Aug. 26, '62,	Mustered out with company, May 29, 1865.
Thomas Canevin	do	Aug. 26, '62,	Pr. to Cor., Nov. 1, 1863 – disch. by G. O. June 16, '65.
Milton S. Lohr	do	Aug. 26, '62,	Pr. to Cor. Nov. 1, '63 mus. out with Co. May 29, '65.
Henry Gibson	do	Aug. 26, '62,	Wounded at Fredericksburg, Va., December 13, 1862—discharged on Surgeon's certificate, May 5, 1863.
George W. Stacy	do	Aug. 26, '62,	Pr. to Cor. April 1, 1864 -disch. by G. O. May 15, 1865.
Peter G. Mathews	do	Aug. 26, '62,	Killed at Gettysburg, Pa., July 1, 1863.
Cyrus Walter	do	Aug. 26, '62,	Died of wounds rec'd at Gettysburg, Pa., July 1, 1863.
Cyrus Swartz	Musician	Aug. 28, '62,	Discharged on Surgeon's certificate, Feb. 27, 1863.
William P. Clark	do	Aug. 28, '62,	Promoted to Principal Musician, March 1, 1864.
Anderson, Clifford	Private	Aug. 26, '62,	Mustered out with company, May 29, 1865.
Aspy, Ezra	do	Aug. 26, '62,	Discharged on Surgeon's certificate, January 20, 1863.

Name.	Rank.	Mustered into Service.	Remarks.
Ash, Thaddeus	Private..	Aug. 26, '62,	Killed at North Anna River, May 23, 1863—buried in Nat. Cem., Richmond, Va., sec 6, div. 3, grave 40.
Brothers, Frank	do	Aug. 26, '62,	Mustered out with company, May 29, 1865.
Buttermore, William	do	Aug. 28, '62,	Mustered out with company, May 29. 1865.
Blake, Wesley	do	Aug. 26, '62,	Mustered out with company, May 29, 1865.
Brier, George	do	Aug. 28, '62,	Mustered out with company, May 29, 1865.
Brothers, Geo. W	do	Aug. 28, '62,	Mustered out with company, May 29, 1865.
Brinker, Simon P	do	Aug. 26, '62,	Mustered out with company, May 29, 1865.
Beal, William S	do	Aug. 26, '62,	Mustered out with company, May 29, 1865.
Byers, Harrison	do	Aug. 26, '62,	Discharged on Surgeon's certificate, Feb. 14, 1863.
Bare, Adam G.	do	Aug. 26, '62,	Discharged on Surgeon's certificate, March 16, 1863.
Berg, Samuel	do	Aug. 26, '62,	Discharged on Surgeon's certificate, August 12, 1864.
Brothers, Cyrus	do	Aug. 26, '62,	Discharged on Surgeon's certificate, Dec. 24, 1864.
Bostler, Manuel	do	Aug. 26, '62,	Died Dec. 29, of wounds rec. at Fredericksburg, Va., Dec. 13, 1862-- buried in Mil. Asy. Cem., D. C.
Coleman, George W.	do	Aug. 26, '62,	Discharged on Surgeon's certificate, Nov. 9, 1863.
Cole, Cyrus	do	Aug. 26, '62,	Tr. to Veteran Reserve Corps, September 25, 1863.
Campbell, John G.	do	Aug. 26, '62,	Tr. to Veteran Reserve Corps, September 25, 1863.
Cunningham, G W	do	Aug. 26, '62,	Killed at Fredericksburg, Va., Dec. 13, 1862.
Cramer, Enos R	do	Aug. 26, '62,	Killed at Gettysburg, Pa., July 1, 1863.
Culp, John.	do	Aug. 26, '62,	Died of wounds received at Fredericksburg, Va., December 13, 1862.
Cramer, Adam G	do	Aug. 26, '62,	Killed at Gettysburg, Pa., July 1, 1863.
Cramer, Samuel	do	Aug. 26, '62,	Killed at Gettysburg, Pa., July 1, 1863—buried in National Cemetery, section B, grave 62.
Durstein, Henry S.	do	Aug. 26, '62,	Discharged on Surgeon's certificate, Dec. 22, 1863.
Ebersole, John W	do	Aug. 26, '62,	Tr. to Veteran Reserve Corps, May 3, 1864.
Finefrock, Samuel	do	Aug. 26, '62,	Killed at Gettysburg, Pa., July 1, 1863.
Gallatin, Albert	do	Aug. 26, '62,	Mustered out with company, May 29, 1865.
Guist, William	do	Aug. 26, '62,	Discharged on Surgeon's certificate, Dec. 17, 1862.
Gettuma, Noah	do	Aug. 26, '62,	Tr. to Vetaran Reserve Corps, November 25, 1863.
House, Joseph	do	Aug. 26, '62,	Mustered out with company, May 29, 1865.
Hanger, Harrison	do	Aug. 26, '62,	Mustered out with company, May 29, 1865.
Hokenshell, David	do	Aug. 26, '62,	Mustered out with company, May 29, 1865.
Horner, Myers	do	Aug. 26, '62,	Mustered out with company, May 29, 1865.
Hartman, John	do	Aug. 26, '62,	Discharged on Surgeon's certificate, Jan. 28, 1863.
Hurst, William Y	do	Aug. 26, '62,	Discharged on Surgeon's certificate, Dec. 7, 1863.
Hokenshell, Samuel	do	Aug. 26, '62,	Tr. to Veteran Reserve Corps, Feb. 15, 1863.
Hays, Abraham H	do	Aug. 26, '62,	Died Jan. 13, 1863, of wounds received at Fredericksburg, Va., Dec. 13, 1862.
Hubbs, James	do	Aug. 28, '62,	Died Jan. 18—burial rec. Jan. 12, 1863—of wounds rec. at Fredericksburg, Va., Dec. 13, 1862—buried in Military Asylum Cemetery, D. C.
Keihl, Amos	do	Aug. 26, '62,	Mustered out with company, May 29, 1865.
Kelly, Charles C	do	Aug. 28, '62,	Mustered out with company, May 29, 1865.
Kowen, Samuel	do	Aug. 26, '62,	Mustered out with company, May 29, 1865.
Kepple, Michael G	do	Aug. 26, '62,	Died at Washington, D. C., Jan. 24, 1864—buried in Military Asylum Cemetery.
Loucks, Martin S	do	Aug. 26, '62,	Mustered out with company, May 29, 1865.
Leaher, Jacob C	do	Aug. 26, '62,	Tr. to Veteran Reserve Corps, Feb. 15, 1863.
Marmie, Peter	do	Aug. 26, '62,	Mustered out with company, May 29, 1865.
Moody, John N.	do	Aug. 26, '62,	Mustered out with company, May 29, 1865.
Malone, Shephard	do	Aug. 26, '62,	Mustered out with company, May 29, 1865. *
Muman, Daniel	do	Aug. 26, '62,	Discharged on Surgeon's certificate, Dec. 20, 1864.
Music, Samuel	do	Aug. 26, '62,	Transferred to Veteran Reserve Corps, Jan. 7, 1863—discharged by General Order, July 5, 1865.
Music, Philip	do	Aug. 26, '62,	Died at Belle Plain, Va., January 1, 1863, of wounds received at Fredericksburg, Dec. 13, 1862.
May, Levi B.	do	Aug. 26, '62,	Killed at Gettysburg, Pa., July 1, 1863.
Niderhiser, Samuel	do	Aug. 26, '62,	Mustered out with company, May 29, 1865.
Nickols, Oliver	do	Aug. 26, '62,	Wounded at Petersburg, Va., June 18, 1864—absent, in hospital, at muster out.
Nidrow, Thomas	do	Aug. 26, '62,	Discharged on Surgeon's certificate, Feb. 24, 1863.
Pool, Alexander	do	Aug. 26, '62,	Mustered out with company, May 29, 1865.
Rowen, Peter	do	Aug. 26, '62,	Mustered out with company, May 29, 1865.
Ruff, Israel M.	do	Aug. 26, '62,	Discharged on Surgeon's certificate, Dec. 27, 1863.
Reese, John W.	do	Aug. 26, '62,	Discharged on Surgeon's certificate, March 2, 1863.
Sullenbarger, George	do	Aug. 26, '62,	Mustered out with company, May 29, 1865.
Sible, Jacob	do	Aug. 26, '62,	Discharged on Surgeon's certificate, Jan. 26, 1863.
Sharrow, Daniel	do	Aug. 26, '62,	Discharged on Surgeon's certificate, Sept. 25, 1863.
Shunk, Benjamin	do	Aug. 26, '62,	Killed at Fredericksburg, Va., Dec. 13, 1862.
Smith, Samuel M	do	Aug. 26, '62,	Died January 16, 1863—burial record, Jan. 9, 1863—of wounds received at Fredericksburg, Va., Dec. 13, 1862—buried in Military Asylum Cemetery, D. C.

ONE HUNDRED AND FORTY-SECOND REGIMENT.

Name.	Rank.	Mustered into Service.	Remarks.
Sullenbarger, Leo'd.	Private.	Aug. 26, '62,	Discharged on Surgeon's certificate, Sept. 25, 1863.
Sims, William	do	Aug. 26, '62,	Died July 24, 1863.
Swain, Franklin	do	Aug. 26, '62,	Killed at Gettysburg, Pa., July 1, 1863.
Sharron, Israel	do	Aug. 26, '62,	Died at Washington, D. C., April 21, 1865—buried in National Cemetery, Arlington, Va.
Thompson, John	do	Aug. 26, '62,	Mustered out with company, May 29, 1865.
Thomas, Samuel	do	Aug. 26, '62,	Mustered out with company, May 29, 1865.
Vance, Joshua	do	Aug. 26, '62,	Mustered out with company, May 29, 1865.
Weaver, John	do	Aug. 26, '62,	Discharged by General Order, July 15, 1865.
Wilkins, Jacob	do	Aug. 28, '62,	Mustered out with company, May 29, 1865.
Washabach, Jacob	do	Aug. 28, '62,	Discharged on Surgeon's certificate, March 25, 1863.
Waltz, Jacob B.	do	Aug. 26, '62,	Killed at Gettysburg, Pa., July 1, 1863.
Zuck, David	do	Aug. 26, '62,	Discharged on Surgeon's certificate, Feb. 9, 1863.

COMPANY C.

Name.	Rank.	Mustered into Service.	Remarks.
John H. Boyts	Captain	Aug. 27, '62,	Discharged on Surgeon's certificate, Feb. 22, 1863.
Henry G. Elder	do	Aug. 27, '62,	Pr. fr. 1st Lt. Feb. 22, 1863- Bv. Maj. March 3, 1865— Bv. Lt. Col. April 2, 1865 wd. at Five Forks, Va., April 1, 1865— com. Major, May 16, 1865 not mus.— mustered out with company, May 29, 1865.
Jacob R. Walter	1st Lt.	Aug. 27, '62,	Pr. from 2d Lieut. Feb. 22, 1863- com. Captain not mustered—wd. at Gettysburg, Pa., July 1, 1863— mustered out with company, May 29, 1865.
Nath. O. Hinchman	2d Lt	Aug. 25, '62,	Pr. from Sgt. June 2, 1863 discharged March 23, 1864.
Charles F. Hunter	1st Sgt	Aug. 25, '62,	Pr. to 1st Sgt. March 1, 1864 com. 1st Lt. not mustered—mustered out with company, May 29, 1865.
John J. Hoffman	do	Aug. 25, '62,	Discharged Dec. 28, 1863.
Franklin Boyts	Sergeant	Aug. 25, '62,	Wounded at Wilderness, Va., May 5, 1864 absent, in hospital, at muster out.
Daniel Young	do	Aug. 25, '62,	Com. 2d Lt. not mus. disch. by G. O., May 25, 1865.
Jacob Phillipi	do	Aug. 25, '62,	Mustered out with company, May 29, 1865.
Benj. F. Harcomb	do	Aug. 25, '62,	Discharged Feb. 25, 1863.
Augustus Davis	do	Aug. 25, '62,	Disch. for wds. rec. at Gettysburg, Pa., July 1, 1863.
Samuel H. Brougher	do	Aug. 25, '62,	Died at Philadelphia, Pa., April 4, 1865.
Norman Phillippi	Corporal	Aug. 25, '62,	Mustered out with company, May 29, 1865.
Wesley Humbert	do	Aug. 25, '62,	Wounded at Gettysburg, Pa., July 1, 1863 tr. to 50th Co., 2d Batt. V. R. C.—disch. by G. O., April 20, '65.
Samuel Gerhart	do	Aug. 25, '62,	Captured at Wilderness, Va., May 5, 1864—died at Andersonville, Ga., Sept. 17, 1864 grave 9005.
Simon Pile	do	Aug. 25, '62,	Mustered out with company, May 29, 1865.
Jonas Mayers	do	Aug. 25, '62,	Mustered out with company, May 29, 1865.
Jacob Bitner	do	Aug. 25, '62,	Mustered out with company, May 29, 1865.
Jacob S. Nichelson	do	Aug. 26, '62,	Discharged Jan. 27, 1863.
Jerome B. Knable	do	Aug. 25, '62,	Transferred to Vet. Res. Corps, Dec. 13, 1863.
Joseph Bitner	do	Aug. 25, '62,	Killed at Gettysburg, Pa., July 1, 1863.
George Snyder	Musician	Aug. 25, '62,	Transferred to Vet. Res. Corps, Dec. 31, 1863.
Charles Elder	do	Aug. 25, '62,	Died December 26, 1862.
Ansell, Michael	Private	Aug. 25, '62,	Mustered out with company, May 29, 1865.
Ansell, David	do	Aug. 25, '62,	Killed at Fredericksburg, Va., Dec. 13, 1862.
Boyts, Benjamin	do	Aug. 25, '62,	Mustered out with company, May 29, 1865.
Bowlby, Samuel	do	Aug. 25, '62,	Discharged Feb. 18, 1863.
Berkey, Elijah H	do	Aug. 25, '62,	Died Jan. 5, 1863— buried in Mil. Asy. Cemetery, D. C.
Boyts, Hiram	do	Aug. 25, '62,	Died at Washington, D. C., Aug. 28, 1864.
Beyers, John	do	Aug. 25, '62,	Died October 24, 1862—buried in National Cemetery, Antietam, Md., section 26, lot C, grave 214.
Cunningham, J. C.	do	Aug. 25, '62,	Tr. to Co. B, 14th reg. Vet. Res. Corps, July 24, 1863— discharged by General Order, June 26, 1865.
Cupp, Hiram	do	Aug. 25, '62,	Killed at Gettysburg, Pa., July 1, 1863.
Cupp, Isaiah	do	Aug. 25, '62,	Died September 12, 1862.
Dumbauld, Frederick	do	Aug. 25, '62,	Mustered out with company, May 29, 1865.
Forespring, Garret	do	Aug. 25, '62,	Mustered out with company, May 29, 1865.
Faith, William	do	Aug. 26, '62,	Discharged February 26, 1863.
Firestone, Michael A.	do	Aug. 25, '62,	Tr. to 95th Co., 2d batt., Vet. Reserve Corps, Dec. 17, 1863– discharged by General Order, Aug. 24, 1865.
Gray, Henry	do	Aug. 30, '64,	Mustered out with company, May 20, 1865.
Growall, Anthony	do	Aug. 25, '62,	Tr. to 160th Co., 2d batt., Vet. Reserve Corps, Feb. 15, 1864 discharged by General Order, July 3, 1865.
Growall, Peter	do	Aug. 26, '62,	Died December 16, 1862.
Henry, Joshua	do	Aug. 25, '62,	Mustered out with company, May 29, 1865.

Name.	Rank.	Mustered into Service.	Remarks.
Hart, Jacob	Private.	Aug. 25, '62,	Mustered out with company, May 29, 1865.
Heinbaugh, John	...do...	Aug. 26, '62,	Mustered out with company, May 29, 1865.
Hoover, John	...do...	Aug. 25, '62,	Wounded at Wilderness, Va., May 5, 1864—discharged by General Order, June 2, 1865.
Hartman, Aaron P.	...do...	Aug. 25, '62,	Mustered out with company, May 29, 1865.
Horner, Daniel J.	...do...	Aug. 25, '62,	Discharged February 23, 1864.
Harsberger, Jacob	...do...	Aug. 25, '62,	Transferred to Co. I, 22d reg. V. R. C., Oct. 17, 1864—discharged by General Order, July 3, 1865.
Hemminger, Alex.	...do...	Aug. 25, '62,	Killed at Fredericksburg, Va., December 13, 1862.
Kimmel, John	...do...	Aug. 25, '62,	Mustered out with company, May 29, 1865.
Kreger, Jacob	...do...	Aug. 25, '62,	Discharged April 22, 1863.
King, Harrison	...do...	Aug. 25, '62,	Killed at Fredericksburg, Va., December 13, 1862.
Levingston, J. W.	...do...	Aug. 25, '62,	Mustered out with company, May 29, 1865.
Levingston, Levi	...do...	Aug. 25, '62,	Wounded at Gettysburg, Pa., July 1, 1863—transferred to V. R. C.—discharged July 17, 1865.
Lee, Perry	...do...	Aug. 26, '62,	Died May 27, 1864.
Miller, Gillian	...do...	Aug. 25, '62,	Mustered out with company, May 29, 1865.
Miner, Martin	...do...	Aug. 25, '62,	Mustered out with company, May 29, 1865.
Moore, Peter	...do...	Aug. 25, '62,	Mustered out with company, May 29, 1865.
Miller, Daniel J	...do...	Aug. 25, '62,	Transferred to Co. D, 18th reg. V. R. C., July 27, 1863—discharged by General Order, June 29, 1865.
May, Daniel	...do...	Aug. 25, '62,	Died February 14, 1863.
Markel, Ringold	...do...	Aug. 25, '62,	Killed at Petersburg, Va., April 2, 1865—buried in Poplar Grove Nat. Cem., div. D, sec. B, grave 43.
Nedrow, Joseph	...do...	Aug. 25, '62,	Mustered out with company, May 29, 1865.
Nicola, Samuel	...do...	Aug. 25, '62,	Absent, in hospital, at muster out.
Nicola, Simon	...do...	Aug. 25, '62,	Missing in action at Wilderness, Va., May 5, 1864.
Nickolson, Adam	...do...	Aug. 26, '62,	Mustered out with company, May 29, 1865.
Nickler, William	...do...	Aug. 26, '62,	Died at Alexandria, Va., of wounds received at Fredericksburg, December 13, 1862.
Nickler, David	...do...	Aug. 25, '62,	Deserted July 22, 1863.
Pile, Peter	...do...	Aug. 25, '62,	Absent, in hospital, at muster out.
Pile, George	...do...	Aug. 25, '62,	Mustered out with company, May 29, 1865.
Pile, William	...do...	Aug. 25, '62,	Discharged January 26, 1864.
Prutts, Jacob	...do...	Aug. 25, '62,	Transferred to 96th Co., 2d batt., V. R. C., Dec. 17, 1863—discharged by General Order, Aug. 24, 1865.
Rector, Washington	...do...	Aug. 25, '62,	Mustered out with company, May 29, 1865.
Rose, Jackson	...do...	Aug. 25, '62,	Discharged December 23, 1863.
Rayman, Jeremiah	...do...	Aug. 25, '62,	Transferred to Vet. Reserve Corps, Feb. 15, 1864.
Rose, Henry	...do...	Aug. 25, '62,	Transferred to Co. II, 10th reg. V. R. C., Jan. 18, 1864—discharged by General Order, June 27, 1865.
Rose, John	...do...	Aug. 25, '62,	Died December 30, 1862.
Shelly, Samuel	...do...	Aug. 25, '62,	Mustered out with company, May 29, 1865.
Shaulis, Simon	...do...	Aug. 25, '62,	Mustered out with company, May 29, 1865.
Stutzman, Elias	...do...	Aug. 25, '62,	Mustered out with company, May 29, 1865.
Sullivan, Irvin	...do...	Aug. 25, '62,	Mustered out with company, May 29, 1865.
Smith, David	...do...	Aug. 25, '62,	Deserted October 2, 1862.
Trimpey, John	...do...	Aug. 25, '62,	Mustered out with company, May 29, 1865.
Vought, John	...do...	Aug. 25, '62,	Died January 11, 1864.
Wable, Foster C.	...do...	Aug. 25, '62,	Wounded at Wilderness, Va., May 5, 1864—discharged by General Order, June 9, 1865.
Welfley, Peter	...do...	Aug. 25, '62,	Mustered out with company, May 29, 1865.
Weimer, David	...do...	Aug. 25, '62,	Killed at Fredericksburg, Va., December 13, 1862.
Yoder, Samuel B.	...do...	Aug. 26, '62,	Disch. for wds. rec'd at Gettysburg, Pa., July 1, 1863.
Zufal, Aaron	...do...	Aug. 26, '62,	Mustered out with company, May 29, 1865.
Zufal, Jacob	...do...	Aug. 26, '62,	Discharged for wounds received at Fredericksburg, Va., December 13, 1862.

Company D.

Name	Rank	Mustered into Service	Remarks
Adam Grimm	Captain.	Aug. 29, '62,	Wounded at Gettysburg, Pa., July 1, 1863—discharged on Surgeon's certificate, April 17, 1864.
Noah Bowman	do..	Aug. 22, '62,	Pr. to Sgt., August 27, 1862—to 1st Sgt., Feb. 1, 1863—to 1st Lt., July 31, 1864—to Captain, Sept. 21, 1864—wounded at Five Forks, Va., April 1, 1865—absent, in hospital, at muster out.
Samuel S. Swank	1st Lt.	Aug. 29, '62,	Wounded at Gettysburg, Pa., July 1, 1863—discharged by special order, February 12, 1864.
Noah S. Miller	do...	Aug. 25, '62,	Pr. to 1st Sgt., Aug. 27, 1862—to 2d Lt., Jan. 11, 1863—to 1st Lt. March 5, 1864—com. Captain, April 20, 1864—not mustered—discharged by G. O., July 30, 1864.

ONE HUNDRED AND FORTY-SECOND REGIMENT.

Name.	Rank.	Mustered into Service.	Remarks.
Charles H. Ferner	1st Lt.	Aug. 27, '62,	Pr. to Sergt. August 27, 1862 to 1st Sgt. Aug. 1, 1864—to 1st Lieut. Sept. 21, 1864 mustered out with company, May 29, 1865.
Henry Stewart	2d Lt.	Aug. 20, '62,	Discharged January 10, 1863.
Oliver P. Shaver	1st Sgt.	Aug. 22, '62,	Pr. to Corporal, Aug. 27, 1862—to Sgt. Feb. 1, 1863—to 1st Sergt. Jan. 1, 1865—com. 2d Lieut. not mustered—mustered out with company, May 29, 1865.
W. E. Zimmerman	Sergeant	Aug. 22, '62,	Pr. to Cor. August 27, 1862—to Sergt. Nov. 12, 1862—mustered out with company, May 29, 1865.
James F. Stanton	do	Aug. 22, '62,	Pr. to Sergt. Aug. 27, 1862—captured at Chapel C. H., Va., October 1, 1864—discharged by General Order, June 13, 1865.
Noah Koontz	do	Aug. 22, '62,	Pr. to Corporal, March 12, 1863 to Sgt. Nov. 1, 1864 mustered out with company, May 29, 1865.
Jacob G. Mishler	Corporal	Aug. 22, '62,	Pr. to Cor. Mar. 12, 1863—absent, sick, at muster out.
Henry Mishler	do	Aug. 22, '62,	Pr. to Cor. June 30, 1863—wounded at Dabney's Mills, Va., Feb. 6, 1865—discharged by G. O., May 13, 1865.
Adam Shafer	do	Aug. 22, '62,	Pr. to Cor. June 30, 1863—absent, sick, at muster out.
David Gohn	do	Aug. 23, '62,	Pr. to Cor. Nov. 1, 1864—wounded at Dabney's Mills, Va., Feb. 6, 1865—absent, sick, at muster out.
Wm. A. Johnson	do	Aug. 23, '62,	Promoted to Corporal, August 27, 1862—discharged on Surgeon's certificate, Dec. 8, 1864.
Charles Lohr	do	Aug. 22, '62,	Promoted to Corporal, August 27, 1862—discharged on Surgeon's certificate, April 8, 1863.
David J. Levingston	do	Aug. 22, '62,	Pr. to Cor. June 30, 1863—disch. date unknown—for wounds received at Gettysburg, Pa., July 1, 1863.
Jacob Barnt	do	Aug. 22, '62,	Pr. to Cor. Sept. 1, 1863—died at Washington, D. C., June 3, of wds. rec'd at Wilderness, Va., May 5, '64.
Isaac Miller	do	Aug. 27, '62,	Promoted to Corporal, Mar. 12, 1863—missing in action at Gettysburg, Pa., July 1, 1863.
Noah W. Shafer	do	Aug. 22, '62,	Promoted to Corporal—date unknown—missing in action at Fredericksburg, Va., Dec. 13, 1862.
Isaac N. Dibert	Musician	Aug. 22, '62,	Absent, on detached service, at muster out.
Dallas M. Unger	do	Aug. 25, '62,	Deserted October 26, 1862.
Ackerman, George	Private.	Aug. 22, '62,	Absent, on detached service, at muster out.
Bissell, Emanuel	do	Aug. 22, '62,	Mustered out with company, May 29, 1865.
Bissell, John H.	do	Aug. 22, '62,	Absent, on detached service, at muster out.
Barnt, Charles	do	Aug. 22, '62,	Mustered out with company, May 29, 1865.
Boyer, John	do	Aug. 22, '62,	Discharged on Surgeon's certificate, March 24, 1863 burial record, died April 6, 1863—buried in Military Asylum Cemetery, D. C.
Barnt, Levi	do	Aug. 22, '62,	Transferred to Veteran Reserve Corps, June 1, 1864.
Berkey, Joseph	do	Aug. 27, '62,	Missing in action at Fredericksburg, Va., Dec. 13, '62.
Berkey, Obiah	do	Aug. 27, '62,	Deserted September 3, 1862.
Barnt, Perry	do		Never mustered.
Caldenbaugh, Jos.	do	Aug. 27, '62,	Absent, on detached service, at muster out.
Custer, Adam	do	Aug. 22, '62,	Tr. to Co. C, 18th regiment V. R. C.—discharged by General Order, July 10, 1865.
Crissey, Hezekiah	do	Aug. 27, '62,	Mustered out with company, May 29, 1865.
Custer, Jonas	do	Aug. 23, '62,	Discharged on Surgeon's certificate, June 1, 1863.
Cook, Pirls	do	Aug. 22, '62,	Tr. to Co. A, 1st regiment V. R. C., May 22, 1863 discharged by General Order, July 14, 1865.
Delany, Daniel	do	Aug. 22, '62,	Mustered out with company, May 29, 1865.
Dull, George	do	Aug. 22, '62,	Mustered out with company, May 29, 1865.
Dickey, John	do	Aug. 27, '62,	Discharged on Surgeon's certificate, June 4, 1863.
Farrel, Leonard	do	Aug. 22, '62,	Absent, on detached service, at muster out.
Fry, Jeremiah	do	Aug. 22, '62,	Mustered out with company, May 29, 1865.
Gohn, Noah	do	Aug. 22, '62,	Died February 14, 1863.
Griffith, Wesley	do	Aug. 22, '62,	Died at Smoketown, Md., Dec. 16, 1862—buried in National Cemetery, Antietam, section 26, lot B, grave 215.
Helsel, Edward	do	Aug. 22, '62,	Mustered out with company, May 29, 1865.
Horner, Henry	do	Aug. 22, '62,	Mustered out with company, May 29, 1865.
Helsel, Martin	do	Aug. 27, '62,	Died at Washington, D. C., Jan. 11, '63—burial record, Dec. 24, 1862—buried in Military Asylum Cemetery.
Hammer, Joseph D.	do	Aug. 22, '62,	Wounded at Gettysburg, Pa., July 1, 1863 died Sept. 9, 1863—buried in National Cemetery, Louden Park, Baltimore, Md.
Kimmel, Rash	do	Aug. 22, '62,	Deserted October 4, 1862.
Lohr, Harrison	do	Aug. 22, '62,	Mustered out with company, May 29, 1865.
Lohr, Benjamin	do	Aug. 22, '62,	Transferred to Vet. Reserve Corps, Nov. 28, 1863.
Lohr, George	do	Aug. 22, '62,	Died July 31, of wounds received at Gettysburg, Pa., July 1, 1863.
Lohr, Josiah	do	Aug. 27, '62,	Deserted September 25, 1862.

ONE HUNDRED AND FORTY-SECOND REGIMENT.

Name.	Rank.	Mustered into Service.	Remarks.
Miller, Isaiah	Private	Aug. 22, '62,	Absent, on detached service, at muster out.
Miller, Samuel J.	do	Aug. 22, '62,	Discharged on Surgeon's certificate, Dec. 18, 1862.
Miller, Josiah	do	Aug. 27, '62,	Discharged on Surgeon's certificate, May 14, 1863.
Miller, Christian M.	do	Aug. 22, '62,	Transferred to V. R. C., Nov. 7, 1864.
Minor, Ephraim	do	Aug. 27, '62,	Transferred to V. R. C., October 17, 1864
Miller, Henry J.	do	Aug. 22, '62,	Transferred to Signal Corps, Nov. 10 1863.
Miller, Rene	do	Aug. 22, '62,	Died November 19, 1864.
Miller, Joseph	do	Aug. 22, '62,	Killed at Hatcher's Run, Va., Oct. 27, 1864.
Miller, Gillian	do	Aug. 22, '62,	Died July 29, of wounds received at Gettysburg, Pa., July 1, 1863.
M'Kinley, Lee H.	do	Aug. 22, '62,	Died Aug. 10, of wounds received at Gettysburg, Pa., July 1, 1863.
Pepley, David	do	Aug. 22, '62,	Killed at Petersburg, Va., June 24, 1864.
Rushenberger, Jno.	do	Aug. 22, '62,	Mustered out with company, May 29, 1865.
Ringler, Harrison	do	Aug. 22, '62,	Absent, on detached service, at muster out.
Reel, John	do	Aug. 22, '62,	Absent, on detached service, at muster out.
Rodgers, William	do	Aug. 22, '62,	Mustered out with company, May 29, 1865.
Rodgers, Franklin	do	Aug. 22, '62,	Absent, on detached service, at muster out.
Ripple, Valentine	do	Aug. 27, '62,	Mustered out with company, May 29, 1865.
Rininger, William	do	Aug. 22, '62,	Tr. to Co. F, 18th reg. Veteran Reserve Corps, June 1, 1864—disch. by General Order, June 27, 1865.
Suter, William	do	Aug. 22, '62,	Absent, on detached service, at muster out.
Speicher, William J.	do	Aug. 27, '62,	Discharged by General Order, June 20, 1865.
Swank, Jacob	do	Aug. 22, '62,	Mustered out with company, May 29, 1865.
Summers, Joshua	do	Aug. 22, '62,	Wounded at Dabney's Mills, February 6, 1865—absent, in hospital, at muster out.
Shafer, Adam B.	do	Aug. 22, '62,	Discharged on Surgeon's certificate, March 24, 1863.
Summers, Michael	do	Aug. 22, '62,	Transferred to Veteran Reserve Corps, May 10, 1864.
Statler, Hiram H.	do	Aug. 22, '62,	Died July 2, of wounds received at Gettysburg, Pa., July 1, 1863.
Sipe, Jacob	do	Aug. 22, '62,	Died at Washington, D. C., Jan. 17, 1863—buried in Military Asylum Cemetery.
Specht, Joseph	do	Aug. 27, '62,	Missing in action at Gettysburg, Pa., July 1, 1863.
Thomas, George C.	do	Aug. 22, '62,	Tr. to Veteran Reserve Corps—date unknown.
Taft, James W.	do	Aug. 22, '62,	Died July 31, of wounds received at Gettysburg, Pa., July 1, 1863—buried in Nat. Cem., sec. B, grave 76.
Woods, John E.	do	Aug. 22, '62,	Mustered out with company, May 29, 1865.
Wilt, Jeremiah	do	Aug. 22, '62,	Deserted September 25, 1862.
Yoder, Isaac	do	Aug. 22, '62,	Died at Belle Plain, Va., February 16, 1863.

COMPANY E.

Name	Rank	Mustered into Service	Remarks
John A. Owens	Captain	Aug. 30, '62,	Discharged on Surgeon's certificate, Feb. 29, 1864.
Charles R. Evans	do	Aug. 30, '62,	Pr. fr. 1st Lt. March 21, 1863—wd. at Gettysburg, Pa., July 1, 1863—mus. out with company, May 29, 1865.
Andrew G. Tucker	1st Lt.	Aug. 30, '62,	Promoted from 2d Lieut. March 21, 1863 died July 5, of wounds received at Gettysburg, Pa., July 1, 1863.
Isaac S. Kerstetter	do	Aug. 28, '62,	Pr. to 1st Sergt. Oct. 20, 1862—to 2d Lieut. April 10, 1863 to 1st Lieut. Nov. 16, 1863—mustered out with company, May 29, 1865.
Scott Clingan	1st Sgt.	Aug. 28, '62,	Pr. to 1st Sergt. April 10, 1863 com. 2d Lieut. July 2, 1863 not mus. wounded at Gettysburg, Pa., July 1, 1863 mustered out with company, May 29, 1865.
Alfred Hayes	do	Aug. 28, '62,	Discharged on Surgeon's certificate, Oct. 22, 1862.
Samuel Brown	Sergeant	Aug. 28, '62,	Promoted to Sergeant, October 29, 1862—mustered out with company, May 29, 1865.
John V. Miller	do	Aug. 28, '62,	Pr. to Sergt. Oct. 29, 1862—wounded at Cold Harbor, Va., June 2, '64 mustered out with Co., May 29, '65.
Reuben B. Fessler	do	Aug. 28, '62,	Pr. to Sgt. June 1, 1863 mus. out with Co. May 29, '65.
Thos. P. Wagner	do	Aug. 28, '62,	Captured at Chapel C. H., Va., October 1, 1864—discharged by General Order, May 29, 1865.
Thomas R. Orwig	do	Aug. 28, '62,	Died at Washington, D. C., November 30, 1862.
Isaac J. Kerstetter	Corporal	Aug. 28, '62,	Pr. to Cor. Oct. 29, 1862—wd. at Spottsylvania C. H., Va., May 12, '64—mus. out with Co., May 29, 1865.
Isaac F. Brown	do	Aug. 28, '62,	Pr. to Cor. Oct. 29, 1862—wd. at Fredericksburg, Va., Dec. 13, 1862—mustered out with Co., May 29, 1865.
John Gellinger	do	Aug. 28, '62,	Pr. to Cor. March, 1864—mus. out with Co. May 29, '65.
Benj. W. Minium	do	Aug. 28, '62,	Promoted to Corporal, June 8, 1864—mustered out with company, May 29, 1865.
Henry C. Penny	do	Aug. 28, '62,	Captured at Chapel C. H., Va., October 1, 1864—discharged by General Order, May 29, 1865.

ONE HUNDRED AND FORTY-SECOND REGIMENT.

Name.	Rank.	Mustered into Service.	Remarks.
John H. Martin	Corporal	Aug. 28, '62,	Disch. Jan. 8, 1863, for wounds received at Fredericksburg, Va., Dec. 13, 1862.
William Keifer	....do...	Aug. 28, '62,	Wounded at Gettysburg, Pa., July 1, 1863—tr. to Veteran Reserve Corps, March 18, 1864.
Nathaniel Strahan	....do...	Aug. 28, '62,	Tr. to Veteran Reserve Corps, Sept. 30, 1863.
Henry M. Speicht	....do...	Aug. 28, '62,	Wounded at Gettysburg, Pa., July 1, 1863—tr. to Veteran Reserve Corps, February 15, 1864.
Jacob H. Rankes	....do...	Aug. 28, '62,	Died June 1, of wounds received at Spottsylvania C. H., Va., May 12, 1864—buried in National Cemetery, Arlington.
Samuel Moyer	....do...	Aug. 28, '62,	Killed at Fredericksburg, Va., Dec. 13, 1862.
William Geibel	Musician	Aug. 28, '62,	Mustered out with company, May 29, 1865.
Hunter B. Barton	....do...	Aug. 28, '62,	Discharged on Surgeon's certificate, May 16, 1863.
Ammon, William L.	Private..	Aug. 28, '62,	Discharged January 16, 1865, for wounds received at Wilderness, Va., May 6, 1864.
Armagast, Peter	....do...	Aug. 28, '62,	Killed at Fredericksburg, Va., Dec. 13, 1862.
Baker, George	....do...	Aug. 28, '62,	Wounded at North Anna River, Va., May 23, 1864- absent, in hospital, at muster out.
Boyer, Solomon	....do...	Aug. 28, '62,	Wounded at Fredericksburg, Va., Dec. 13, 1862, and at Spottsylvania C. H., May 10, 1864—mustered out with company, May 20, 1865.
Boope, George E.	....do...	Aug. 28, '62,	Transferred to 51st company, 2d battalion, Veteran Reserve Corps, November 15, 1863 discharged by General Order, Aug. 28, 1865.
Campbell, Reuben	....do...	Aug. 28, '62,	Mustered out with company, May 29, 1865.
Donachy, William L.	....do...	Aug. 28, '62,	Mustered out with company, May 29, 1865.
Deibert, John P.	....do...	Aug. 28, '62,	Killed at Catlett's Station, Va., Nov. 30, 1863.
Dellinger, John S.	....do...	Aug. 28, '62,	Killed at Fredericksburg, Va., December 13, 1862.
Fetter, Adam	....do...	Aug. 28, '62,	Mustered out with company, May 29, 1865.
Fangboner, Theo.	....do...	Aug. 28, '62,	Mustered out with company, May 29, 1865.
Fullmer, William H.	....do...	Aug. 28, '62,	Mustered out with company, May 29, 1865.
Fees, David	....do...	Aug. 28, '62,	Mustered out with company, May 29, 1865.
Farley, John	....do...	Aug. 28, '62,	Discharged April 8, 1864, for wounds received at Fredericksburg, Va., December 13, 1862.
Fetler, David	....do...	Aug. 28, '62,	Died of wounds received at Fredericksburg, Va., December 13, 1862.
Gellinger, Jackson	....do...	Aug. 28, '62,	Mustered out with company, May 29, 1865.
Gibboney, Jacob B.	....do...	Aug. 28, '62,	Discharged on Surgeon's certificate, May 10, 1863.
Gundy, James P.	....do...	Aug. 28, '62,	Discharged May 5, 1863, for wounds received at Fredericksburg, Va., Dec. 13, 1862.
Hoffman, Noah	....do...	Aug. 28, '62,	Mustered out with company, May 29, 1865.
Hoffman, Henry W.	....do...	Aug. 28, '62,	Mustered out with company, May 29, 1865.
Hoffman, John	....do...	Aug. 28, '62,	Mustered out with company, May 29, 1865.
Hartman, Har'n R.	....do...	Aug. 28, '62,	Discharged February 28, 1863, for wounds received at Fredericksburg, Va., Dec. 13, 1862.
Hoffman, Solomon B.	....do...	Aug. 28, '62,	Discharged April 13, 1864, for wounds received at Fredericksburg, Va., December 13, 1862.
Houghton, Thomas	....do...	Aug. 28, '62,	Wounded at Gettysburg, Pa., July 1, 1863 discharged on Surgeon's certificate, September 4, 1864.
Jamison, David	....do...	Aug. 28, '62,	Died of wounds received at Fredericksburg, Va., December 13, 1862.
Koser, Uriah	....do...	Aug. 28, '62,	Discharged April 9, 1863, for wounds received at Fredericksburg, Va., December 13, 1862.
Koser, William	....do...	Aug. 28, '62,	Died at Warrenton, Va., November, 1862.
Kline, John	....do...	Aug. 28, '62,	Died of wounds received at Wilderness, Va., May 6, 1864.
Kling, John	....do...	Aug. 28, '62,	Died at Acquia Creek, Va., Jan. 22, 1863.
LeFevre, Frank P.	....do...	Aug. 28, '62,	Mustered out with company, May 29, 1865.
Lenhart, Jacob	....do...	Aug. 28, '62,	Discharged on Surgeon's certificate, Feb. 19, 1864.
Marr, James	....do...	Aug. 28, '62,	Mustered out with company, May 29, 1865.
Moyer, John N.	....do...	Aug. 28, '62,	Discharged January 29, 1863, for wounds received at Fredericksburg, Va., December 13, 1862.
Moser, Jacob	....do...	Aug. 28, '62,	Killed at Cold Harbor, Va., June 1, 1864.
Moser, Jeremiah	....do...	Aug. 28, '62,	Died of wounds received at Fredericksburg, Va., December 13, 1862.
Martin, Henry	....do...	Aug. 28, '62,	Died at Sharpsburg, Md., Nov. 24, 1862—buried in National Cemetery, Antietam, section 26, lot B, grave 224.
Martin, Daniel	....do...	Aug. 28, '62,	Died of wounds received at Fredericksburg, Va., December 13, 1862.
Moyer, Levi B.	....do...	Aug. 28, '62,	Died of wounds received at Fredericksburg, Va., December 13, 1862.
Minium, John A.	....do...	Aug. 28, '62,	Captured at Wilderness, Va., May 5, 1864.
Morris, A. Judson	....do...	Aug. 28, '62,	Dropped from rolls—date unknown.

Name.	Rank.	Mustered into Service.	Remarks.
M'Bride, Daniel	Private	Aug. 28, '62,	Discharged January 24, 1863, for wounds received at Fredericksburg, Va., December 13, 1862.
Pontius, Henry B.	do	Aug. 28, '62,	Mustered out with company, May 29, 1865.
Reichley, George	do	Aug. 28, '62,	Mustered out with company, May 29, 1865.
Reish, George	do	Aug. 28, '62,	Mustered out with company, May 29, 1865.
Raboss, John	do	Aug. 28, '62,	Discharged Feb. 26, 1865, for wounds received at Petersburg, Va., June, 1864.
Rank, Samuel	do	Aug. 28, '62,	Discharged on Surgeon's certificate, Dec. 14, 1863.
Renner, William I.	do	Aug. 28, '62,	Discharged on Surgeon's certificate, Feb. 4, 1863.
Raboss, Henry	do	Aug. 28, '62,	Accidentally killed, March 24, 1865—buried in Poplar Grove, National Cemetery, Petersburg, Va., division C, section H, grave 31.
Renner, Levi	do	Aug. 28, '62,	Died at Richmond, Va., February 23, 1863, of wounds received at Fredericksburg, Va., Dec. 13, 1862.
Root, David	do	Aug. 28, '62,	Died at Gettysburg, Pa., July 3, 1863.
Smith, Henry M.	do	Aug. 28, '62,	Wounded at Chapel C. H., Va., Oct. 1, 1864—mustered out with company, May 29, 1865.
Sechler, William R.	do	Aug. 28, '62,	Wounded at Spottsylvania C. H., Va., May 10, 1864—mustered out with company, May 29, 1865.
Shaffer, Jeremiah	do	Aug. 28, '62,	Mustered out with company, May 29, 1865.
Showalter, John W.	do	Aug. 28, '62,	Mustered out with company, May 29, 1865.
Steinmetz, Philip	do	Aug. 28, '62,	Discharged May 9, 1863, for wounds received at Fredericksburg, Va., December 13, 1862.
Smith, Henry C.	do	Aug. 28, '62,	Discharged on Surgeon's certificate, Feb. 20, 1863.
Smith, Michael	do	Aug. 28, '62,	Discharged on Surgeon's certificate, Feb. 9, 1864.
Graham, James C	do	Aug. 28, '62,	Discharged on Surgeon's certificate, Feb. 19, 1863.
Shields, William	do	Aug. 28, '62,	Promoted to Sergeant Major, March 1, 1864.
Stettler, Henry	do	Aug. 28, '62,	Died at Washington, D. C., October 12, 1862—burial record, Oct. 7, 1864—buried in Military Asylum Cem.
Stapleton, George	do	Aug. 28, '62,	Died July 26, of wounds received at Gettysburg, Pa., July 1, 1863.
Stuck, Henry	do	Aug. 28, '62,	Died of wounds received at Fredericksburg, Va., December 13, 1862.
Stitzer, Samuel	do	Aug. 28, '62,	Died at Washington, D. C., May 30, of wounds received at North Anna River, Va., May 23, 1864—buried in National Cemetery, Arlington.
Sortman, Daniel	do	Aug. 28, '62,	Deserted December 15, 1862.
Wolfe, Emanuel	do	Aug. 28, '62,	Mustered out with company, May 29, 1865.
Wilson, Robert M.	do	Aug. 28, '62,	Wounded at Fredericksburg, Va., December 13, 1862—mustered out with company, May 29, 1865.
Wolfe, William H.	do	Aug. 28, '62,	Wounded at Fredericksburg, Va., December 13, 1862—transferred to Vet. Res. Corps, July 21, 1863.
Wynn, Thomas	do	Aug. 28, '62,	Deserted December 15, 1862.

Company F.

Name.	Rank.	Mustered into Service.	Remarks.
Fran's A. Edmonds	Captain	Aug. 25, '62,	Discharged November 1, 1862.
Albert Heffley	do	Aug. 25, '62,	Pr. fr. 1st Lt., Nov. 1, '62—disch. by G. O., May 19, '65.
Josiah Lepley	1st Lt.	Aug. 25, '62,	Promoted from private, April 9, 1863—com. Capt.—not mus.—mus. out with company, May 29, 1865.
George J. Gordill	2d Lt.	Aug. 25, '62,	Com. 1st Lt. Nov. 1, '62 not mus.—disch. Mar. 11, '63, for wds. rec'd at Fredericksburg, Va., Dec. 13, 1862.
Cyrus P. Heffley	do	Aug. 25, '62,	Pr. fr. Cor. to Sgt. Sept. 1, '62—to 2d Lt. Apr. 10, 1865—captured—returned—wounded at Gettysburg, Pa., July 1, 1863—discharged by S. O., May 15, 1865.
Jacob J. Zorn	1st Sgt.	Aug. 25, '62,	Pr. fr. Sgt. May 25, 1864—com. 1st Lt.—not mustered—mustered out with company, May 29, 1865.
Jacob B. Lepley	do	Aug. 25, '62,	Died May 24, of wounds received at Wilderness, Va., May 5, 1864.
John Denton	Sergeant	Aug. 25, '62,	Mustered out with company, May 29, 1865.
Martin Caton	do	Aug. 25, '62,	Mustered out with company, May 29, 1865.
Samuel Houn	do	Aug. 25, '62,	Pr. fr. Cor. Nov. 27, 1863—com. 2d Lt. - not mustered—mustered out with company, May 29, 1865.
Parker Diveley	do	Aug. 25, '62,	Pr. to Cor. November 27, 1863—to Sgt. Oct. 22, 1864—mustered out with company, May 29, 1865.
Joseph Smith	do	Aug. 25, '62,	Deserted October 1, 1862.
Jacob Wellington	Corporal	Aug. 25, '62,	Pr. to Cor. Nov. 27, 1863—pris. from May 5, 1864, to Feb. 28, 1865—discharged by G. O. June 5, 1865.
Henry Stuck	do	Aug. 25, '62,	Pr. to Cor. Oct. 22, '64—mus. out with Co., May 29, '65.

ONE HUNDRED AND FORTY-SECOND REGIMENT. 75

Name.	Rank.	Mustered into Service.	Remarks.
Benjamin Hay	Corporal	Aug. 29, '62,	Pr. to Cor. Oct. 22, 1864—wounded at Five Forks, Va., April 1, 1865—discharged by G. O., June 3, 1865.
Samuel Boose	do	Aug. 25, '62,	Discharged on Surgeon's certificate, Nov. 17, 1862.
Chauncey Dickey	do	Aug. 25, '62,	Pr. to Cor. Nov. 27, 1863—disch. by G. O., May 17, '6
Adam Cook	do	Aug. 25, '62,	Tr. to Veteran Reserve Corps, July 27, 1863.
Samuel J. Bittner	do	Aug. 25, '62,	Transferred to Company D, 11th reg. V. R. C., May 1864—discharged by General Order, July 7, 1865.
Hermon Fritz	do	Aug. 25, '62,	Died December 14, of wounds received at Fredericks burg, Va., Dec. 13, 1862.
Henry Bittner	do	Aug. 25, '62,	Died at Warrenton, Va., November 14, 1862.
Hiram Sturtz	do	Aug. 25, '62,	Killed at Fredericksburg, Va., Dec. 13, 1862.
Christopher Speicher	do	Aug. 25, '62,	Deserted January 21, 1863.
Hermon Johnson	Musici'n	Aug. 25, '62,	Mustered out with company, May 29, 1865.
Charles Flato	do	Aug. 25, '62,	Mustered out with company, May 29, 1865.
William H. Platte	do	Aug. 25, '62,	Discharged on Surgeon's certificate, March 19, 1863.
Atchison, William	Private	Aug. 25, '62,	Captured—died at Andersonville, Ga., Jan. 25, 1865—grave 12520.
Bowman, Chauncey	do	Aug. 25, '62,	Mustered out with company, May 29, 1865.
Beal, Jacob N.	do	Aug. 25, '62,	Absent, sick, at muster out.
Blachart, Jeremiah	do	Sept. 9, '64,	Discharged on Surgeon's certificate, Dec. 13, 1864.
Bridegum, Henry	do	Aug. 25, '62,	Tr. to Veteran Reserve Corps—date unknown.
Bisel, Benjamin	do	Aug. 25, '62,	Captured—died at Andersonville, Ga., Oct. 22, 1864 grave 11222.
Braugher, Jeremiah	do	Aug. 25, '62,	Deserted January 20, 1863.
Broucher, Gillian	do	Aug. 29, '62,	Deserted January 20, 1863.
Boyer, Anthony	do	Sept. 18, '62,	Transferred to Vet. Reserve Corps—date unknown discharged by General Order, June 20, 1865.
Christner, Jacob	do	Aug. 25, '62,	Mustered out with company, May 29, 1865.
Caton, William	do	Sept. 9, '64,	Discharged on Surgeon's certificate, Dec. 13, 1864.
Caton, Elias	do	Aug. 25, '62,	Killed at Fredericksburg, Va., Dec. 13, 1862.
Coleman, Francis	do	Aug. 26, '62,	Killed at Spottsylvania C. H., Va., May 11, 1864.
Dickey, William	do	Aug. 25, '62,	Mustered out with company, May 29, 1865.
Dickey, Alexander	do	Aug. 25, '62,	Transferred to Co. K, 14th reg. Vet. R. C.—date unknown—disch. by General Order, June 28, 1865.
Exline, Emanuel	do	Aug. 25, '62,	Discharged on Surgeon's certificate, Dec. 7, 1865.
Fogle, George	do	Aug. 25, '62,	Mustered out with company, May 29, 1865.
Fisher, Tobias	do	Aug. 25, '62,	Prisoner from August 21, 1864, to March 2, 1865—discharged by General Order, June 6, 1865.
Fritz, Uriah	do	Aug. 29, '62,	Captured at Gettysburg, Pa., July , 1863—died at Andersonville, Ga., Oct. 19, 1864.
Glessner, George	do	Aug. 25, '62,	Discharged by General Order, May 25, 1865.
Griffith, Andrew	do	Aug. 25, '62,	Discharged on Surgeon's certificate, Mar. 16, 1863.
Groff, John A	do	Aug. 25, '62,	Transferred to Veteran Reserve Corps, July 24, 1863.
Heffley, Zacharias	do	Aug. 25, '62,	Mustered out with company, May 29, 1865.
Heckman, Daniel	do	Aug. 25, '62,	Discharged on Surgeon's certificate, March 9, 1863.
Hay, John	do	Aug. 25, '62,	Discharged by General Order, May 17, 1865.
Hoover, Charles	do	Aug. 25, '62,	Discharged by General Order, May 17, 1865.
Hittie, William	do	Aug. 25, '62,	Discharged on Surgeon's certificate, Sept. 12, 1863.
Hay, Henry	do	Aug. 25, '62,	Tr. to Co. F, 9th reg. Vet. Res. Corps, Nov. 29, 1863—discharged by General Order, June 26, 1865.
Hogle, Francis	do	Aug. 25, '62,	Transferred to Veteran Reserve Corps, July 24, 1863.
Hartz, Henry	do	Aug. 25, '62,	Tr. to Co. I, 4th reg. Vet. Res. Corps, Jan. 21, 1865 discharged by General Order, July 15, 1865.
Hentz, William	do	Aug. 25, '62,	Tr. to Co. B, 14th reg. Vet. Res. Corps, Sept. 18, 1864 —discharged by General Order, July 21, 1865.
Hersh, Francis	do	Aug. 29, '62,	Killed at Fredericksburg, Va., December 13, 1862.
Keller, Joshua	do	Aug. 25, '62,	Captured—died at Andersonville, Ga., Oct. 10, 1864 bu. in Lawton Nat. Cem., Millen, sec. A, grave 274.
Keller, Justus	do	Aug. 25, '62,	Transferred to Signal Corps, October, 1863.
Leidig, William M	do	Aug. 25, '62,	Mustered out with company, May 29, 1865.
Leidig, Jonathan	do	Aug. 25, '62,	Transferred to Veteran Reserve Corps, Jan. 1, 1865.
Murdic, Alexander	do	Aug. 25, '62,	Mustered out with company, May 29, 1865.
Mosholder, Joseph	do	Aug. 25, '62,	Mustered out with company, May 29, 1865.
Muhlenberg, Chas.	do	Aug. 25, '62,	Mustered out with company, May 29, 1865.
Miller, Charles	do	Aug. 25, '62,	Discharged on Surgeon's certificate, July 7, 1864.
Mason, Joseph F	do	Aug. 25, '62,	Promoted to Hospital Steward, May 1, 1863.
Mull, Peter	do	Aug. 25, '62,	Died at Brooks' Station, Va., Nov. 25, 1862.
Miller, Joseph	do	Aug. 29, '62,	Deserted October 1, 1862.
Parker, Andrew	do	Aug. 25, '62,	Killed at Dabney's Mills, Va., February 6, 1865.
Queer, Levi	do	Aug. 25, '62,	Mustered out with company, May 29, 1865.
Ringler, Alexander	do	Aug. 25, '62,	Mustered out with company, May 29, 1865.
Rumiser, Henry	do	Aug. 25, '62,	Tr to Co. C, 24th reg. Vet. Res. Corps, July 1, 1864—discharged by General Order, June 28, 1865.
Rayman, William	do	Aug. 25, '62,	Killed at Dabney's Mills, Va., February 6, 1865.

Name.	Rank.	Mustered into Service.	Remarks.
Ream, Michael	Private.	Aug. 25, '62,	Tr. to 169th Co., 2d batt., V. R. Corps, Mar. 27, 1864—discharged by General Order, July 3, 1865.
Ream, Joseph	do	Aug. 25, '62,	Killed at Gettysburg, Pa., July 1, 1863.
Suder, Henry	do	Aug. 29, '62,	Absent, sick, at muster out.
Shoemaker, James	do	Aug. 25, '62,	Mustered out with company, May 29, 1865.
Spangy, William	do	Aug. 25, '62,	Mustered out with company, May 29, 1865.
Sweitzer, James	do	Aug. 25, '62,	Mustered out with company, May 29, 1865.
Shoemaker, Anan's	do	Aug. 25, '62,	Mustered out with company, May 29, 1865.
Sellers, Augustus	do	Aug. 25, '62,	Mustered out with company, May 29, 1865.
Steinberg, Moses	do	Aug. 25, '62,	Mustered out with company, May 29, 1865.
Scritchfield, Jesse	do	Aug. 25, '62,	Mustered out with company, May 29, 1865.
Shafer, John	do	Aug. 20, '62,	Mustered out with company, May 20, 1865.
Sivits, Joseph	do	Aug. 25, '62,	Killed at Gettysburg, Pa., July 1, 1863.
Stewart, Henry	do	Aug. 25, '62,	Deserted Nov. 18, 1862.
Schram, Henry	do	Aug. 25, '62,	Deserted October 1, 1862.
Steiner, John	do	Aug. 25, '62,	Deserted August 25, 1863.
Slaybauch, Henry	do	Sept. 9, '64,	Never joined company.
Walker, Zachariah	do	Aug. 25, '62,	Absent, sick, at muster out.
Walker, Joseph	do	Aug. 25, '62,	Mustered out with company, May 29, 1865.
Weimer, John	do	Aug. 25, '62,	Mustered out with company, May 29, 1865.
Will, Charles J.	do	Aug. 25, '62,	Mustered out with company, May 29, 1865.
Will, George	do	Aug. 25, '62,	Tr. to Co. D, 18th reg. V. R. Corps, August 15, 1863—discharged by General Order, June 29, 1865.
Wolford, John	do	Aug. 25, '62,	Tr. to Co. B, 11th reg. Vet. Res. Corps, Sept 19, 1864—discharged by General Order, July 13, 1865.
Ware, Henry	do	Aug. 29, '62,	Transferred to Vet. Reserve Corps, March 28, 1865—discharged by General Order, July 28, 1865.

Company G.

Name	Rank	Mustered into Service	Remarks
Wm. K. Haviland.	Captain	Aug. 31, '62,	Transferred to 14th reg. Vet. Reserve Corps, May 1, 1863—discharged August 20, 1866.
Cicero H. Drake.	do	Aug. 31, '62,	Pr. from Sgt. to 2d Lt. April 1, 1863—to Capt. May 13, 1865—mustered out with company, May 29, 1865.
Charles P. Orvis.	1st Lt.	Aug. 31, '62,	Com. Captain, Dec. 14, 1863—not mustered—promoted to Adjutant, December 19, 1863.
B. T. Huntsman.	do	Aug. 31, '62,	Promoted from Sergeant to 1st Lieut. May 3, 1864—mustered out with company, May 29, 1865.
George La Bar	2d Lt.	Aug. 31, '62,	Discharged by special order, October 24, 1862.
Josiah Heckman	1st Sgt	Aug. 31, '62,	Pr. to Cor. May 29, 1863—to Sgt. Dec. 30, 1863—to 1st Sergt. Feb. 6, 1865—com. 2d Lieut.—not mustered—mustered out with company, May 29, 1865.
Amzi La Bar	do	Aug. 31, '62,	Discharged on Surgeon's certificate, July 1, 1863.
Jacob F. William	do	Aug. 31, '62,	Pr. to Sergt. May 25, 1863—to 1st Sgt. June 30, 1864—killed at Dabney's Mills, Va., February 6, 1865.
Aaron Smith	Sergeant	Aug. 31, '62,	Pr. to Cor. May 29, 1863—to Sergt. October 31, 1864—mustered out with company, May 29, 1865.
Levi C. Drake	do	Aug. 31, '62,	Pr. to Cor. Dec. 30, 1863—to Sergeant Oct. 31, 1864—mustered out with company, May 29, 1865.
John R. Miller	do	Aug. 31, '62,	Pr. to Cor. March 18, 1864—to Sergeant Feb. 28, 1865—mustered out with company, May 29, 1865.
Jackson Eberitt	do	Aug. 31, '62,	Discharged January 22, 1865, for wounds received at North Anna River, Va., May 23, 1864.
Peter F. Wagner	Corporal	Aug. 31, '62,	Pr. to Cor. Oct. 31, '64 mus. out with Co., May 29, '65.
Justus Gimble	do	Aug. 31, '62,	Transferred to Veteran Reserve Corps, Nov. 13, 1863.
Henry Palmer	do	Aug. 31, '62,	Pr. to Cor. May 25, 1863—wounded at Gettysburg, Pa., July 1, 1863—tr. to 3d Co., 2d batt., V. R. C.—date unknown—discharged August 16, 1865.
Matthew G. Allegar.	do	Aug. 31, '62,	Pr. to Cor. May 25, 1863—died August 6, of wounds received at Gettysburg, Pa., July 1, 1863.
Edward Brandis	do	Aug. 31, '62,	Killed at Fredericksburg, Va., December 13, 1862.
Jas. D. Connelly.	do	Aug. 31, '62,	Promoted to Corporal, May 25, 1863—killed at Gettysburg, Pa., July 1, 1863.
Theodore Fenner	do	Aug. 31, '62,	Died at Washington, D. C., Jan. 12, 1863, of wounds received at Fredericksburg, Va., December 13, 1862—buried in Military Asylum Cemetery.
James Ferguson	do	Aug. 31, '62,	Died at Washington, D. C., Jan. 29, 1863, of wounds received at Fredericksburg, Va., Dec. 13, 1862.
Jervis Ney	do	Aug. 31, '62,	Killed at Fredericksburg, Va., Dec. 13, 1862.
N. S. Vanauken	do	Aug. 31, '62,	Died at Brooks' Station, Va., Nov. 25, 1862.

ONE HUNDRED AND FORTY-SECOND REGIMENT. 77

Name.	Rank.	Mustered into Service.	Remarks.
Oliver Pitney	Corporal	Aug. 31, '62,	Deserted December 8, 1863.
John B. Lawrence	Musician	Aug. 31, '62,	Mustered out with company, May 29, 1865.
Silas Hanna	do	Aug. 31, '62,	Mustered out with company, May 29, 1865.
Arnst, James D.	Private	Aug. 31, '62,	Mustered out with company, May 29, 1865.
Amick, Daniel	do	Sept. 16, '62,	Discharged by special order, Sept. 9, 1864.
Blowers, Elijah	do	Aug. 31, '62,	Mustered out with company, May 29, 1865.
Benson, Peter	do	Aug. 31, '62,	Mustered out with company, May 29, 1865.
Bellis, Linford D.	do	Aug. 31, '62,	Wounded at Dabney's Mills, Va., Feb. 6, 1865—absent, in hospital, at muster out.
Bellis, Lewis	do	Aug. 31, '62,	Wounded at Fredericksburg, Va., December 13, 1862 absent, sick, at muster out.
Bradshaw, James	do	Aug. 31, '62,	Discharged on Surgeon's certificate, May 2, 1863.
Burch, Edwin	do	Aug. 31, '62,	Tr. to Co. D, 11th reg. V. R. C., November 13, 1863 discharged by General Order, July 7, 1865.
Bensley, Charles	do	Aug. 31, '62,	Died at Washington, D. C., January 12, 1863—buried in Military Asylum Cemetery.
Bellis, Amos	do	Aug. 31, '62,	Killed at Fredericksburg, Va., Dec. 13, 1862.
Compton, John	do	Aug. 31, '62,	Discharged on Surgeon's certificate, Feb. 11, 1863
Countryman, Dan'l	do	Aug. 31, '62,	Tr. to 75th Co., 2d batt., V. R. C., September 23, 1864 discharged by General Order, June 28, 1865.
Crock, William T.	do	Aug. 31, '62,	Captured—died at Annapolis, Md., Dec. 30, 1864.
Connelly, Philip D.	do	Aug. 31, '62,	Deserted July, 1863.
Delong, Elmer H.	do	Aug. 31, '62,	Killed at Fredericksburg, Va., Dec. 13, 1862.
Devitt, William D.	do	Aug. 31, '62,	Killed at Fredericksburg, Va., December 13, 1862.
Ebernt, Edwin R.	do	Aug. 31, '62,	Wounded at Dabney's Mills, Va., Feb. 6, 1865 absent, in hospital, at muster out.
Feller, Balser	do	Aug. 31, '62,	Discharged on Surgeon's certificate, June 2, 1863.
Frable, James	do	Aug. 31, '62,	Killed at Fredericksburg, Va., Dec. 13, 1862.
Fenner, Jeffrey	do	Aug. 31, '62,	Died—date unknown.
Gearhart, Edwin R.	do	Aug. 31, '62,	Transferred to Signal Corps—date unknown.
Garris, Amos	do	Aug. 31, '62,	Died at Alexandria, Va., January 12, 1863, of wounds rec'd at Fredericksburg, Dec. 13, 1862—grave 070.
Hoover, James	do	Aug. 31, '62,	Mustered out with company, May 29, 1865.
Howey, Moses	do	Mar. 16, '64,	Transferred to 190th regiment P. V., May 29, 1865.
Howey, Amos	do	Mar. 16, '64,	Transferred to 190th regiment P. V., May 29, 1865.
Huff, James	do	Mar. 16, '64,	Transferred to 190th regiment P. V., May 29, 1865 discharged by General Order, June 10, 1865.
Hull, Benjamin	do	Aug. 31, '62,	Killed at Fredericksburg, Va., December 13, 1862.
Hickman, Jos. F.	do	Aug. 31, '62,	Died—date unknown.
Jaggers, Joseph L.	do	Aug. 31, '62,	Killed at Gettysburg, Pa., July 1, 1863.
Knecht, Jacob	do	Aug. 31, '62,	Captured at Boydton Plank Road, Va., Mar. 31, 1865 discharged by General Order, June 3, 1865.
Kresge, Steward	do	Aug. 31, '62,	Discharged October 25, 1864, for wounds received at Gettysburg, Pa., July 1, 1863.
Kresge, Joseph	do	Aug. 31, '62,	Died May 30, of wounds received at Wilderness, Va., May 6, 1864 buried in Nat. Cem., Arlington.
Knecht, Henry	do	Aug. 31, '62,	Missing in action at Wilderness, Va., May 6, 1864.
Layton, Morris H.	do	Aug. 31, '62,	Transferred to Vet. Res. Corps—date unknown.
La Bar, Levi	do	Mar. 16, '64,	Transferred to 190th regiment P. V., May 29, 1865.
La Bar, Linford	do	Aug. 31, '62,	Killed at Fredericksburg, Va., December 13, 1862.
Meeker, David H.	do	Aug. 31, '62,	Wounded at Wilderness, Va., May 5, 1864 absent, in hospital, at muster out.
Metz, John	do	Feb. 24, '64,	Transferred to 190th regiment, P. V., May 29, 1865.
Marsh, Abraham B.	do	Aug. 31, '62,	Transferred to Vet. Reserve Corps, Sept. 30, 1863.
Nuttall, Joseph	do	Aug. 31, '62,	Captured at Gettysburg, Pa., July 1, 1863—wounded at Five Forks, Va., April 1, 1865—mustered out with company, May 29, 1865.
Neauman, Thos. W.	do	Aug. 31, '62,	Mustered out with company, May 29, 1865.
Neauman, Charles	do	Aug. 31, '62,	Killed at Fredericksburg, Va., December 13, 1862.
Overleigh, Albert	do	Aug. 31, '62,	Disch. on Surg. cert., Jan. 12, 1864—re-enlisted March 21, 1864—mis. in action at Wilderness, Va., May 6, 1864—died at Annapolis, Md., Dec. 19, 1864.
Row, Philip	do	Aug. 31, '62,	Mustered out with company, May 29, 1865.
Rinker, Joseph	do	Aug. 31, '62,	Deserted October 9, 1862.
Shinnerling, C. F.	do	Aug. 31, '62,	Mustered out with company May 29, 1865.
Small, John	do	Aug. 31, '62,	Captured at Boydton Plank Road, Va., Mar. 31, 1865 discharged by General Order, June 3, 1865.
Smith, Omer B.	do	Aug. 31, '62,	Mustered out with company, May 29, 1865.
Smith, George, Jr	do	Aug. 31, '62,	Deserted October 9, 1862—returned October 9, 1864 mustered out with company, May 29, 1865.
Stein, Ephraim	do	Aug. 8, '64,	Mustered out with company, May 29, 1865.
Strunk, Theodore	do	Mar. 8, '64,	Transferred to 190th regiment, P. V., May 29, 1865.
Strunk, Jeremiah	do	Aug. 31, '62,	Transferred to 128th Co., 2d batt., V. R. C., June 15, 1864—discharged by General Order, June 29, 1865.

Name.	Rank.	Mustered into Service.	Remarks.
Strunk, Elijah	Private.	Mar. 8, '64,	Transferred to 190th regiment P. V., May 29, 1865.
Smiley, Thomas	...do...	Aug. 31, '62,	Died at Washington, D. C., December 30, of wounds received at Fredericksburg, Va., Dec. 13, 1862.
Shafer, Henry	...do...	Aug. 31, '62,	Died January 2, 1863.
Slutter, Henry	...do...	Aug. 31, '62,	Killed at Gettysburg, Pa., July 1, 1863.
Terry, Charles	...do...	Aug. 31, '62,	Discharged on Surgeon's certificate, Jan. 21, 1863.
Transue, Ananias	...do...	Aug. 31, '62,	Discharged on Surgeon's certificate, Feb. 24, 1863.
Transue, George W.	...do...	Aug. 31, '62,	Died December 22, 1862.
Tittle, Jerome	...do...	Aug. 31, '62,	Deserted—date unknown.
Vanauken, Moses D.	...do...	Aug. 31, '62,	Mustered out with company, May 29, 1865.
Vanrohy, Wm. H.	...do...	Aug. 31, '62,	Transferred to Vet. Reserve Corps, Sept. 22, 1864.
Wallace, Charles B.	...do...	Aug. 31, '62,	Mustered out with company, May 29, 1865.
Woolbert, Jacob	...do...	Aug. 31, '62,	Wounded at Boydton Plank Road, Va., March 31, 1865 —absent, in hospital, at muster out.
Woolbert, Thomas	...do...	Aug. 31, '62,	Mustered out with company, May 29, 1865.
Wilson, James	...do...	Aug. 31, '62,	Transferred to U. S. Navy, March 28, 1864.
Wells, William F.	...do...	Aug. 31, '62,	Transferred to Co. F, 3d reg. Vet. Reserve Corps date unknown—discharged July 6, 1865.
White, Charles S.	...do...	Aug. 31, '62,	Died at Washington, D. C., Jan. 26, 1863, of wounds received at Fredericksburg, Va., Dec. 13, 1862.
Woolbert, Jacob T.	...do...	Aug. 31, '62,	Killed at Fredericksburg, Va., December 13, 1862.

Company H.

Name.	Rank.	Mustered into Service.	Remarks.
Joshua M. Dushane	Captain.	Aug. 18, '62,	Discharged by General Order, May 15, 1865.
Daniel W. Dull	1st Lieut	Aug. 30, '62,	Discharged on Surgeon's certificate, May 26, 1863.
George H. Collins	...do...	Aug. 19, '62,	Pr. from 1st Sergt. to 2d Lt., April 10, 1863—to 1st Lt., June 28, 1863 –killed at Wilderness, Va., May 5, '64.
Isaac Francis, Jr.	do...	Aug. 19, '62,	Promoted from 1st Sergeant to 2d Lieutenant, July 1, 1863—to 1st Lt. June 26, 1864—died at City Point, Va., Feb. 15, 1865, of wounds received in action.
Hugh Cameron	2d Lieut	Aug. 18, '62,	Discharged on Surgeon's certificate, Mar. 7, 1863.
Joseph F. Forrey	1st Sergt	Aug. 19, '62,	Pr. to Cor. June 1, 1863—to Sergt. Mar. 1, 1864—to 1st Sgt. April 1, 1864—mus. out with Co., May 29, 1865.
Wm. F. Kurtz	...do...	Aug. 19, '62,	Killed at Fredericksburg, Va., December 13, 1862.
Samuel Wilson	Sergeant	Aug. 19, '62,	Wounded at Petersburg, Va., April 1, 1865—discharged by General Order, June 3, 1865.
John V. Stouffer	...do...	Aug. 19, '62,	Discharged by General Order, May 17, 1865.
James X. Walter	...do...	Aug. 19, '62,	Pr. to Corporal, Sept. 1, 1864—to Sergeant February 6, 1865—mustered out with company, May 29, 1865.
David B. Hood	...do...	Aug. 19, '62,	Discharged on Surgeon's certificate, March 16, 1863.
Samuel H. Dull	...do...	Aug. 27, '62,	Promoted to Sergeant Major—date unknown.
Robinson Balsley	...do...	Aug. 19, '62,	Transferred to Veteran Reserve Corps, May 1, 1864.
Joseph R. Brown	...do...	Aug. 19, '62,	Transferred to 42d Co., 2d batt., Veteran Reserve Corps, Feb. 1, 1865—discharged Aug. 19, 1865.
Joseph Balsley	...do...	Aug. 19, '62,	Died December 24, of wounds received at Fredericksburg, Va., December 13, 1862.
William Whaley	...do...	Aug. 19, '62,	Died July 27, of wounds received at Gettysburg, Pa., July 1, 1863.
Romanus Dull	...do...	Aug. 19, '62,	Captured—died at Richmond, Va., March 4, 1865.
Frederick Shearer	Corporal	Aug. 19, '62,	Wounded at Petersburg, Va., April 1, 1865—discharged by General Order, June 3, 1865.
James D. Connell	...do...	Aug. 19, '62,	Wounded at Petersburg, Va., March 25, 1865—discharged by General Order, June 3, 1865.
James Mitts	...do...	Aug. 19, '62,	Promoted to Corporal, March 14, 1864—mustered out with company, May 29, 1865.
Levi Firestone	...do...	Aug. 19, '62,	Wounded at Petersburg, Va., Apr. 1, 1865—discharged by General Order, June 27, 1865.
Strickler Demuth	...do...	Aug. 19, '62,	Promoted to Corporal, March 1, 1865—mustered out with company, May 29, 1865.
Richard Evans	...do...	Aug. 19, '62,	Discharged February 26, 1863.
William Helms	...do...	Aug. 19, '62,	Discharged March 10, 1863.
Edward Y. White	...do...	Aug. 19, '62,	Discharged by General Order, May 15, 1865.
William H. Shaw	...do...	Aug. 19, '62,	Tr. to Co. E, 9th reg. V. R. C., October 30, 1863—discharged by General Order, June 29, 1865.
Abraham Eicher	...do...	Aug. 19, '62,	Tr. to Co. D, 11th reg. V. R. C., October 30, 1863—discharged by General Order, July 7, 1865.
Henry Kurtz	...do...	Aug. 19, '62,	Transferred to Vet. Res. Corps, October 17, 1863.
Winfield S. Hood	...do...	Aug. 19, '62,	Tr. to 51st Co., 2d batt., Veteran Reserve Corps, Feb. 2, 1865—discharged by G. O., July 20, 1865.
Josiah R. Balsley	...do...	Aug. 19, '62,	Killed at Fredericksburg, Va., December 13, 1862.

ONE HUNDRED AND FORTY-SECOND REGIMENT.

Name.	Rank.	Mustered into Service.	Remarks.
David R. Gallatin	Corporal	Aug. 19, '62,	Deserted February 8, 1863.
Artis, Jacob	Private	Aug. 26, '62,	Transferred to Vet. Res. Corps, August 1, 1863.
Artis, William A	do	Aug. 19, '62,	Transferred to Vet. Res. Corps, January 1, 1865.
Artis, William	do	Sept. 10, '62,	Killed at Fredericksburg, Va., Dec. 13, 1862.
Balsby, David	do	Aug. 19, '62,	Mustered out with company, May 29, 1865.
Bigham, David	do	Sept. 10, '62,	Mustered out with company, May 29, 1865.
Cooper, Husing	do	Aug. 19, '62,	Discharged by General Order, May 13, 1865.
Collins, Alexander	do	Sept. 2, '62,	Wounded at Gettysburg, Pa., July 1, 1863—absent, in hospital, at muster out.
Clark, Jacob	do	Aug. 19, '62,	Mustered out with company, May 29, 1865.
Coughenour, Jos.	do	Aug. 19, '62,	Discharged December 15, 1862.
Cunningham, Thad.	do	Aug. 19, '62,	Discharged on Surgeon's certificate, March 6, 1863.
Cooley, James	do	Aug. 19, '62,	Killed at Gettysburg, Pa., July 1, 1863.
Dull, Walter	do	Aug. 26, '62,	Mustered out with company, May 29, 1865.
Durbin, Stewart	do	Aug. 19, '62,	Discharged February 9, 1863.
Eaglen, John W	do	Aug. 19, '62,	Died March 11, 1863.
Francis, John C	do	Aug. 19, '62,	Discharged by General Order, June 15, 1865.
Firestone, Hawkins	do	Aug. 19, '62,	Mustered out with company, May 29, 1865.
Freeman, Leroy W	do	Aug. 19, '62,	Died Nov. 11, 1864, of wounds received in action.
Helms, Gibson	do	Aug. 19, '62,	Mustered out with company, May 29, 1865.
Hall, Garrett	do	Sept. 20, '62,	Mustered out with company, May 29, 1865.
Heffly, Samuel	do	Aug. 19, '62,	Discharged June 21, 1863.
Hodge, Josiah	do	Aug. 19, '62,	Died November 20, 1863.
Harvey, William H	do	Aug. 19, '62,	Killed at Gettysburg, Pa., July 1, 1863.
Hart, Joshua M	do	Aug. 19, '62,	Deserted January 1863.
Ingraham, Jesse	do	Aug. 19, '62,	Mustered out with company, May 29, 1865.
Johnston, Lloyd	do	Mar. 30, '64,	Discharged—date unknown.
Johnston, Jos. W	do	Aug. 13, '64,	Killed at Five Forks, Va., April 1, 1865.
Kern, John H	do	Aug. 19, '62,	Mustered out with company, May 29, 1865.
Kimmel, Singleton	do	Aug. 26, '62,	Discharged January 9, 1863.
Kooser, Alexander	do	Sept. 20, '62,	Died November 30, 1862.
Kerr, Isaac	do	Aug. 19, '62,	Killed at Spottsylvania C. H., Va., May 12, 1864.
Loughrey, Henry	do	Aug. 19, '62,	Discharged May, 1865.
Loughrey, John	do	Aug. 26, '62,	Died January 9, 1863.
May, Leonard	do	Aug. 26, '62,	Mustered out with company, May 29, 1865.
Mitts, John	do	Sept. 2, '62,	Mustered out with company, May 29, 1865.
Miller, William	do	Sept. 10, '62,	Mustered out with company, May 29, 1865.
Martin, Frederick	do	Aug. 19, '62,	Discharged March 24, 1864.
Morris, Nathan W	do	Aug. 19, '62,	Transferred to Veteran Reserve Corps, April 27, 1865—discharged by General Order, June 26, 1865.
M'Laughlin, Rob't	do	Aug. 19, '62,	Died June 7, of wounds rec'd at Spottsylvania C. H., Va., May 11, '64—buried at Alexandria, grave 2061.
Nicholson, Henry	do	Aug. 19, '62,	Mustered out with company, May 29, 1865.
Ober, Jacob	do	Aug. 26, '62,	Deserted July 1, 1863.
Porter, Wm. H	do	Aug. 26, '62,	Mustered out with company, May 29, 1865.
Rowen, John	do	Aug. 26, '62,	Mustered out with company, May 29, 1865.
Ridenour, Wm	do	Aug. 26, '62,	Wounded at Gettysburg, Pa., July 1, 1863—absent, in hospital, at muster out.
Rist, Conrad F	do	Aug. 19, '62,	Discharged by General Order, May 15, 1865.
Ridenour, Jeremiah	do	Aug. 26, '62,	Discharged February 28, 1863.
Robbins, Matthew	do	Sept. 2, '62,	Killed at Fredericksburg, Va., Dec. 13, 1862.
Rugg, Gabriel	do	Aug. 19, '62,	Deserted November 4, 1862.
Stoner, Levi	do	Aug. 19, '62,	Wounded at Gettysburg, Pa., July 1, 1863—transferred to Company A, 6th regiment, Vet. Reserve Corps—discharged by General Order, July 6, 1865.
Sheppard, Wm. H	do	Aug. 19, '62,	Transferred to Company F, 6th regiment, Vet. Res. Corps—discharged by General Order, July 10, 1865.
Shisley, Wm	do	Aug. 19, '62,	Discharged by General Order, May 16, 1865.
Saylor, Jacob	do	Sept. 20, '62,	Transferred to Vet. Res. Corps, Sept. 1, 1863.
Stouffer, John B	do	Aug. 19, '62,	Killed at Gettysburg, Pa., July 1, 1863.
Shallenberger, L. W	do	Aug. 19, '62,	Captured—died at Andersonville, Ga., July 22, 1864.
Vance, Clayton	do	Aug. 19, '62,	Discharged January 23, 1863.
Williams, Wm	do	Sept. 20, '62,	Captured at Wilderness, Va., May 5, 1864.
Whitly, Charles H	do	Aug. 19, '62,	Discharged on Surgeon's certificate, March 11, 1863.
Walker, Jacob O	do	Aug. 19, '62,	Discharged February 18, 1863.
Whipkey, Wm. H	do	Sept. 20, '62,	Tr. to Company K, 6th reg. V. R. C., March 15, 1864—discharged July 3, 1865.

COMPANY I.

Name.	Rank.	Mustered into Service.	Remarks.
William Hasson	Captain	Sept. 5, '64,	Wounded at Gettysburg, Pa., July 1, 1863—discharged by special order, October 5, 1863.
Geo. R. Snowden	....do...	Aug. 30, '62,	Pr. from 1st Sergt. to 1st Lt. Sept. 1, 1862— to Captain, Nov. 16, 1863—disch. by special order, Apr. 7, 1864.
Cyrus H. Culver	....do...	Aug. 30, '62,	Pr. to Sgt. Sept. 1, 1862—to 1st Sgt. March 12, 1863—to 1st Lieut. Jan. 15, 1864—to Captain, May 1, 1864—mustered out with company, May 29, 1865.
William H. Rhodes	1st Lieut.	Aug. 30, '62,	Pr. to Sgt. March 12, 1863—to 1st Sgt. June 6, 1864—to 1st Lieut. July 1, 1864—mustered out with company, May 29, 1865.
Charles E. Huston	2d Lieut.	Sept. 1, '62,	Wd. at Gettysburg, Pa., July 1, 1863 dis. Sept. 14, '63.
Oliver P. Young	1st Sergt	Aug. 30, '62,	Pr. from Sgt. to 1st Sgt. July 6, 1864— com. 2d Lieut.—not mustered—mus. out with Co., May 20, 1865.
Abram S. Prather	....do...	Aug. 30, '62,	Discharged on Surgeon's certificate, Jan. 5, 1863.
Thomas Hogue	Sergeant	Aug. 30, '62,	Pr. to Cor. Jan. 22, 1864—to Sergt. July 7, 1864—mustered out with company, May 20, 1865.
Conrad Heasley	....do...	Aug. 30, '62,	Mustered out with company, May 20, 1865.
James K. Elliott	....do...	Aug. 30, '62,	Mustered out with company, May 29, 1865.
Loren M. Fulton	....do...	Aug. 30, '62,	Promoted to Sergt. June 6, 1864— mustered out with company, May 29, 1865.
Johnson W. Kerr	....do...	Aug. 30, '62,	Discharged March 12, 1863.
Wilson Camp	....do...	Aug. 30, '62,	Pr. to Lieut. 8th reg. U. S. C. T., September 8, 1863—to Capt. Feb. 28, 1865—mustered out, Nov. 10, 1865.
William Reynolds	....do...	Aug. 30, '62,	Died of wounds received at Gettysburg, Pa., July 1, 1863—buried in Nat. Cem., section C, grave 36.
Jesse B. Moore	Corporal	Aug. 30, '62,	Mustered out with company, May 20, 1865.
George M. Wingar	....do...	Sept. 5, '62,	Promoted to Corporal, March 12, 1863—wounded at Spottsylvania C. H., Va., May 9, 1864—discharged by General Order, June 3, 1865.
Charles Holbrook	....do...	Aug. 30, '62,	Promoted to Corporal, Oct. 26, 1863—discharged by General Order, June 24, 1865.
Joshua Foster	....do...	Aug. 30, '62,	Promoted to Corporal, June 6, 1864—mustered out with company, May 20, 1865.
John A. Wilcox	....do...	Aug. 30, '62,	Promoted to Corporal, July 12, 1864—mustered out with company, May 29, 1865.
William Gorman	....do...	Aug. 30, '62,	Promoted to Corporal, July 12, 1864—mustered out with company, May 20, 1865.
David S. Keep	....do...	Aug. 30, '62,	Discharged August 30, 1864, for wounds, with loss of leg, received in action.
Artimus Hollis	....do...	Aug. 30, '62,	Killed at Spottsylvania C. H., Va., May 12, 1864.
Daniel Weaver	....do...	Aug. 30, '62,	Killed at North Anna River, Va., May 23, 1864.
John G. M'Lane	Musician	Aug. 30, '62,	Mustered out with company, May 20, 1865.
Best, George	Private	Aug. 30, '62,	Mustered out with company, May 20, 1865.
Bogue, Henry H	....do...	Aug. 30, '62,	Captured at Gettysburg, Pa., July 1, 1863 discharged by General Order, May 26, 1865.
Brown, Samuel	....do...	Aug. 30, '62,	Mustered out with company, May 29, 1865.
Bookster, Martin	....do...	Aug. 30, '62,	Mustered out with company, May 20, 1865.
Bartlebaugh, Philip	....do...	Aug. 30, '62,	Mustered out with company, May 29, 1865.
Bower, William	....do...	Aug. 30, '62,	Mustered out with company, May 20, 1865.
Burgwin, Wesley H	....do...	Aug. 30, '62,	Discharged January 12, 1864, for wounds received at Gettysburg, Pa., July 1, 1863.
Beatty, Eli	....do...	Aug. 30, '62,	Discharged July 11, 1864.
Bower, James	....do...	Aug. 30, '62,	Died at Philadelphia, Pa., July 20, of wounds received at Gettysburg, Pa., July 1, 1863.
Brown, Israel B	....do...	Aug. 30, '62,	Died May 7, of wounds received at Wilderness, Va., May 5, 1864.
Craig, Robert	....do...	Aug. 30, '62,	Mustered out with company, May 29, 1865.
Corbin, George W	....do...	Aug. 30, '62,	Discharged by General Order, July 10, 1865.
Coldrew, David	....do...	Aug. 30, '62,	Mustered out with company, May 29, 1865.
Chesley, Frank W	....do...	Aug. 30, '62,	Discharged March 15, 1863.
Coburn, Joseph H	....do...	Sept. 5, '62,	Discharged April 14, 1863.
Colburn, Samuel J	....do...	Sept. 5, '62,	Died of wounds received at Gettysburg, Pa., July 1, 1863— buried in Nat. Cem., section E, grave 30.
Dempsey, Peter	....do...	Aug. 30, '62,	Mustered out with company, May 29, 1865.
Davis, Richard	....do...	Aug. 30, '62,	Discharged on Surgeon's certificate, Sept. 22, 1863.
Ducket, John	....do...	Aug. 30, '62,	Killed at Spottsylvania C. H., Va., May 12, 1864—buried in Burial Grounds Wilderness.
Dilmore, Jacob	....do...	Aug. 30, '62,	Died at Windmill Point, Va., Feb. 5, 1863.

ONE HUNDRED AND FORTY-SECOND REGIMENT. 81

Name.	Rank.	Mustered into Service.	Remarks.
Downing, Daniel	Private	Aug. 30, '62,	Killed at Wilderness, Va., May 5, 1864.
Egal, Eli	do	Sept. 5, '62,	Mustered out with company, May 29, 1865.
Findley, William K	do	Sept. 5, '62,	Mustered out with company, May 29, 1865.
Finch, Daniel H	do	Aug. 30, '62,	Mustered out with company, May 29, 1865.
Gunderman, Herm'n	do	Aug. 30, '62,	Mustered out with company, May 29, 1865.
Grossman, Simon	do	Aug. 30, '62,	Mustered out with company, May 29, 1865.
Gibbons, John	do	Aug. 30, '62,	Discharged March 2, 1863.
Hatch, Philip M	do	Aug. 30, '62,	Discharged on Surgeon's certificate, Oct. 20, 1863.
Hill, James	do	Aug. 30, '62,	Died of wounds received at Gettysburg, Pa., July 1, 1863 buried in Nat. Cem., section B, grave 27.
Hogue, John W	do	Aug. 30, '62,	Died February 24, 1863.
Hogue, John E	do	Mar. 24, '64,	Deserted July 30, 1864.
James, David	do	Aug. 10, '62,	Discharged by General Order, June 27, 1865.
Jennings, Wise'n W	do	Aug. 30, '62,	Mustered out with company, May 29, 1865.
Kelly, Samuel	do	Sept. 5, '62,	Mustered out with company, May 29, 1865.
Kennedy, Wilson	do	Aug. 30, '62,	Mustered out with company, May 29, 1865.
Keep, Charles E	do	Aug. 30, '62,	Died near Fredericksburg, Va., Dec. 10, 1862.
Little, Jacob F	do	Sept. 5, '62,	Mustered out with company, May 29, 1865.
Laney, William	do	Aug. 30, '62,	Mustered out with company, May 29, 1865.
Lamb, James F	do	Aug. 10, '62,	Absent, sick, at muster out.
Lee, David	do	Aug. 30, '62,	Mustered out with company, May 29, 1865.
Lockwood, Geo. R	do	Aug. 30, '62,	Died of wounds rec'd at Gettysburg, Pa., July 1, 1863.
Mellin, Henry	do	Aug. 30, '62,	Wounded in action—disch. by G. O., June 17, 1865.
Moran, Patrick	do	Aug. 30, '62,	Mustered out with company, May 29, 1865.
Mathews, Gain'l W	do	Aug. 30, '62,	Mustered out with company, May 29, 1865.
Morrison, Samuel	do	Aug. 30, '62,	Discharged Feb. 20, 1863.
Manville, Adrian G	do	Aug. 30, '62,	Transferred to U. S. Navy, April 10, 1864.
M'Cray, Boint	do	Aug. 30, '62,	Mustered out with company, May 29, 1865.
M'Cray, Andrew	do	Aug. 30, '62,	Mustered out with company, May 29, 1865.
M'Fate, Samuel	do	Aug. 30, '62,	Mustered out with company, May 29, 1865.
MacLane, James E	do	Aug. 30, '62,	Tr. to 121st Co., 2d batt., V. R. C., March 2, 1864 discharged on Surgeon's certificate, March 20, 1865.
M'Calmont, H. R	do	Aug. 30, '62,	Transferred to Vet. Res. Corps—date unknown.
M'Naughton, Dan'l	do	Aug. 30, '62,	Died at Alexandria, June 4, of wounds received at Spottsylvania Court House, Va., May 12, 1864 grave 2023.
Nyman, John G. L	do	Aug. 30, '62,	Discharged on Surgeon's certificate, Jan. 16, 1863.
Nicklin, Lambert F	do	Aug. 30, '62,	Killed at Wilderness, Va., May 6, 1864.
Ray, Samuel	do	Aug. 30, '62,	Mustered out with company, May 29, 1865.
Robinson, John	do	Sept. 5, '62,	Deserted May 15, 1863.
Strohman, Henry	do	Aug. 30, '62,	Mustered out with company, May 29, 1865.
Shiffer, John	do	Aug. 30, '62,	Mustered out with company, May 29, 1865.
Stiner, John	do	Aug. 30, '62,	Mustered out with company, May 29, 1865.
Shaw, Hugh	do	Aug. 30, '62,	Mustered out with company, May 29, 1865.
Shirley, Joseph B	do	Sept. 5, '62,	Mustered out with company, May 29, 1865.
Slamon, Owen	do	Aug. 30, '62,	Mustered out with company, May 29, 1865.
Small, Joseph	do	Aug. 30, '62,	Discharged March 15, 1863.
Sheriff, William J	do	Sept. 5, '62,	Discharged January 27, 1864, for wounds received at Gettysburg, Pa., July 1, 1863.
Sharpnack, John W	do	Sept. 5, '62,	Discharged March 15, 1863.
Shaw, James W	do	Aug. 30, '62,	Discharged on Surgeon's certificate, Oct. 7, 1863.
Shirley, Jacob A	do	Sept. 5, '62,	Transferred to Vet. Res. Corps—date unknown.
Siverline, Adam	do	Aug. 30, '62,	Wounded and missing in action at Fredericksburg, Va., Dec. 13, 1862.
Shelmadine, W. W	do	Sept. 5, '62,	Wounded and missing in action at Gettysburg, Pa., July 1, 1863.
Turner, Augustus V	do	Aug. 30, '62,	Killed at Gettysburg, Pa., July 1, 1863.
West, William	do	Aug. 30, '62,	Absent, in hospital, at muster out.
Wesner, Marcus	do	Aug. 30, '62,	Mustered out with company, May 29, 1865.
Walden, Jeremiah	do	Aug. 30, '62,	Mustered out with company, May 29, 1865.
Wadsworth, W. G	do	Aug. 30, '62,	Transferred to 55th company, 2d batt., V. R. C.—date unknown—disch. by G. O., Aug. 29, 1865.
Webber, George P	do	Aug. 30, '62,	Captured at Weldon R. R., Va., August 21, 1864—died at Salisbury, N. C., November 4, 1864.
Wilcox, Josiah	do	Aug. 30, '62,	Deserted May 25, 1863.
Wesner, Wm. B	do	Aug. 30, '62,	Captured—returned—deserted August, 1863.
Yockey, Jacob	do	Sept. 5, '62,	Mustered out with company, May 29, 1865.

COMPANY K.

Name.	Rank.	Mustered into Service.	Remarks.
Charles H. Flagg	Captain	Sept. 1, '62,	Killed at Gettysburg, Pa., July 3, 1863.
Joshua W. Howell	do	Aug. 30, '62,	Promoted from Corporal to Captain, May 1, 1864 mustered out with company, May 29, 1865.
Jeremiah Hoffman	1st Lieut	Sept. 1, '62,	Com. Capt. July 4, 1863—not mus. disch. Nov. 21, for wounds received at Gettysburg, Pa., July 1, 1863.
John W. Dissinger	do	Sept. 2, '62,	Pr. fr. Sgt. Sept. 21, '64 mus. out with Co. May 29, '65.
Cyrus K. Campbell	2d Lieut.	Sept. 1, '62,	Commissioned 1st Lieut. July 4, 1863—not mustered discharged March 9, 1863, for wounds received at Fredericksburg, Va., Dec. 13, 1862.
Samuel Decker	1st Sgt.	Aug. 30, '62,	Pr. to 1st Sergt. Sept. 1, 1864—com. 2d Lt.—not mus.- mustered out with company, May 29, 1865.
Albert G. Ink	do	Aug. 30, '62,	Mis. in action at Fredericksburg, Va., Dec. 13, 1862.
Wm. G. Garrett	do	Sept. 24, '62,	Died Aug. 26, of wounds received at Petersburg, Va., June 18, 1864.
John P. Williams	Sergeant	Aug. 30, '62,	Pr. to Sgt. Oct. 1, 1864—mus. out with Co., May 29, '65.
David R. Samuel	do	Aug. 30, '62,	Discharged on Surgeon's certificate, July 15, 1863.
Solomon W. Strohm.	do	Sept. 1, '62,	Discharged April 27, 1863, for wounds received at Fredericksburg, Va., December 13, 1862.
George W. Brink	do	Aug. 30, '62,	Wounded at Fredericksburg, Va., December 13, 1862— transferred to Company D, 18th reg. V. R. C., Aug. 15, 1863—disch. by General Order, June 29, 1865.
Alpheus Cutler	do	Aug. 30, '62,	Transferred to Vet. Res. Corps, Nov. 15, 1863.
Charles Steel	Corporal	Aug. 30, '62,	Pr. to Cor. Mar. 1, '63—mus. out with Co., May 29, '65.
John P. Griffiths	do	Aug. 30, '62,	Promoted to Corporal, April, 1863—captured at Wilderness, May 5, 1864.
George Strickler	do	Sept. 1, '62,	Pr. to Cor. Feb. 3, '65—mus. out with Co., May 29, '65.
John T. Reed	do	Sept. 1, '62,	Pr. to Cor. Mar. 1, '65—mus. out with Co., May 29, '65.
Martin L. Burtch	do	Aug. 30, '62,	Discharged on Surgeon's certificate, Mar. 1, 1863.
James D. Giddings	do	Aug. 30, '62,	Discharged on Surgeon's certificate, Jan. 16, 1863.
John G. Silkworth	do	Aug. 30, '62,	Discharged on Surgeon's certificate, Jan. 19, 1863.
Edward Mehlman	do	Sept. 1, '62,	Wd. at Gettysburg, Pa., July 1, 1863—tr. to V. R. C., Mar. 1865—disch. by Gen. Order, June 26, 1865.
Isaac Gisner	do	Aug. 30, '62,	Wd. at Gettysburg, Pa., July 1, 1863—tr. to V. R. C.— date unknown—disch. by G. O., June 26, 1865.
Wm. Fastnought	do	Aug. 30, '62,	Died at Frederick, Md., Nov. 16, '62—burial record, Oct. 28, 1862—buried at Mt. Olivet Cemetery.
Nathan Allen	do	Aug. 30, '62,	Pr. to Cor. Aug. 18, 1864—died Feb. 7, at City Point, Va., of wounds rec'd at Dabney's Mill, Feb. 6, 1865.
James V. Staley	do	Sept. 25, '62,	Promoted to Corporal, May 11, 1863—died at Petersburg, Va., Nov. 30, 1864.
Lewis Wagner	do	Aug. 30, '62,	Deserted September, 1862.
Thomas Prothero	Musici'n	Aug. 30, '62,	Mustered out with company, May 29, 1865.
Burkey, Charles K.	Private	Sept. 25, '62,	Mustered out with company, May 29, 1865.
Bevan, Lewis	do	Aug. 30, '62,	Discharged on Surgeon's certificate, Oct., 1862.
Bickel, Abraham	do	Sept. 1, '62,	Discharged on Surgeon's certificate, Dec. 14, 1863.
Bickle, Henry	do	Sept. 1, '62,	Discharged on Surgeon's certificate, April 9, 1864.
Cammer, Chester	do	Aug. 30, '62,	Mustered out with company, May 29, 1865.
Cooper, William	do	Aug. 30, '62,	Discharged on Surgeon's certificate, March 16, 1863.
Cool, John	do	Aug. 30, '62,	Tr. to Co. G, 12th reg. V. R. C., Feb. 11, 1864—discharged by General Order, June 29, 1865.
Conrad, John	do	Aug. 30, '62,	Mis. in action at Fredericksburg, Va., Dec. 13, 1862.
Davis, John R	do	Aug. 30, '62,	Mustered out with company, May 29, 1865.
Davis, Samuel	do	Sept. 1, '62,	Mustered out with company, May 29, 1865.
Decker, Charles	do	Aug. 30, '62,	Mustered out with company, May 29, 1865.
Decker, Oliver	do	Aug. 30, '62,	Discharged February 20, 1863, for wounds received at Fredericksburg, Va., Dec. 13, 1862.
Dunlap, John	do	Aug. 30, '62,	Discharged on Surgeon's certificate, Feb., 1863.
Davis, Youngs	do	Aug. 30, '62,	Transferred to Vet. Res. Corps—date unknown.
Doolebohn, John	do	Sept. 1, '62,	Transferred to Vet. Res. Corps—date unknown.
Donley, James E.	do	Sept. 24, '62,	Transferred to Signal Corps—date unknown.
Dupple, Samuel	do	Sept. 1, '62,	Died July 24, of wds. received at Spottsylvania C. H., Va., May 12, 1864—buried in Nat. Cem., Arlington.
Evans, Watkin	do	Aug. 30, '62,	Mustered out with company, May 29, 1865.
Evans, Jenkin	do	Aug. 30, '62,	Killed at Fredericksburg, Va., Dec. 13, 1862.
Fitzgerald, Edward	do	Aug. 30, '62,	Discharged on Surgeon's certificate, March 15, 1864.
Garrett, Henry M.	do	Sept. 1, '62,	Mustered out with company, May 29, 1865.
Garber, Peter	do	Sept. 1, '62,	Discharged March 24, for wounds received at Fredericksburg, Va., Dec. 13, 1862.
Gisner, Jacob	do	Aug. 30, '62,	Discharged on Surgeon's certificate, Jan. 13, 1864.

ONE HUNDRED AND FORTY-SECOND REGIMENT.

Name.	Rank.	Mustered into Service.	Remarks.
Griest, George	Private	Sept. 1, '62,	Discharged on Surgeon's certificate, Feb. 3, 1863.
Gruver, Thomas	do	Aug. 30, '62,	Discharged on Surgeon's certificate, May 15, 1865.
Hale, Denzimore N.	do	Aug. 30, '62,	Mustered out with company, May 29, 1865.
Hampton, William	do	Aug. 30, '62,	Captured at Petersburg, Va., Jan. 24, 1865 disch. by General Order, May 26, 1865.
Heisey, David	do	Sept. 1, '62,	Mustered out with company, May 29, 1865.
House, John	do	Aug. 30, '62,	Wounded at Fredericksburg, Va., December 13, 1862 absent, in hospital, at muster out.
Holvey, John	do	Aug. 30, '62,	Discharged on Surgeon's certificate—date unknown.
Hass, Merritt	do	Aug. 30, '62,	Transferred to Vet. Reserve Corps, Jan. 1, 1865.
Jones, Wm. D.	do	Aug. 30, '62,	Discharged by special order, Nov. 15, 1864.
Johnson, William	do	Aug. 30, '62,	Deserted December 3, 1862.
Jones, Meredith	do	Aug. 30, '62,	Deserted July 1, 1863.
Kendall, Wm. H.	do	Aug. 30, '62,	Mis. in action at Fredericksburg, Va., Dec. 13, 1862.
Laird, William	do	Aug. 30, '62,	Wounded and captured at Fredericksburg, Va., Dec. 13, 1862—died at Richmond, Jan. 3, 1863.
Lutringer, Benj.	do	Aug. 30, '62,	Wounded and captured at Fredericksburg, Va., Dec. 13, 1862—died at Richmond, Jan. 14, 1863.
Miller, Lewis	do	Sept. 1, '62,	Wounded at Dabney's Mills, Va., February 6, 1865—discharged by General Order, June 7, 1865.
Meredith, Thomas	do	Aug. 30, '62,	Discharged March 4, 1863, for wounds received at Fredericksburg, Va., December 13, 1862.
Morgan, John	do	Aug. 30, '62,	Discharged January 23, 1863.
Morris, Reuben	do	Aug. 30, '62,	Discharged January 13, 1863.
M'Lean, John	do	Sept. 1, '62,	Discharged on Surgeon's certificate, Mar. 24, 1863.
M'Camley, Zuray	do	Aug. 30, '62,	Killed at Fredericksburg, Va., Dec. 13, 1862.
M'Nellis, Barney	do	Aug. 30, '62,	Deserted—date unknown.
Nagle, John S.	do	Feb. 3, '65,	Transferred to 190th reg. P. V., May 29, 1865.
Peters, William	do	Sept. 1, '62,	Mustered out with company, May 29, 1865.
Phillipi, William	do	Sept. 1, '62,	Missing in action at Gettysburg, Pa., July 1, 1863.
Smith, Samuel	do	Sept. 1, '62,	Mustered out with company, May 29, 1865.
Steinmetz, George	do	Sept. 1, '62,	Mustered out with company, May 29, 1865.
Seiders, Michael	do	Sept. 1, '62,	Prisoner from May 5, 1864, to May 14, 1865—mustered out with company, May 29, 1865.
Souders, Jacob	do	Sept. 1, '62,	Discharged by special order, Sept. 15, 1864.
Seagrist, Jonas	do	Sept. 1, '62,	Wounded at Gettysburg, Pa., July 1, 1863—transferred to Veteran Reserve Corps, January 1, 1865.
Seiders, William H	do	Sept. 2, '62,	Transferred to Co. A, 6th reg. Vet. Reserve Corps, Jan. 15, 1864—disch. by General Order, July 6, 1865.
Shortz, Lewis	do	Aug. 30, '62,	Transferred to Veteran Reserve Corps, Feb. 15, 1864.
Scott, George C.	do	Aug. 30, '62,	Wounded and captured at Fredericksburg, Va., Dec. 13, 1862—died at Annapolis, Md., Feb. 22, 1863.
Seiders, John	do	Sept. 1, '62,	Captured—died at Andersonville, Ga., July 19, 1864—grave 3632.
Smith, Henry	do	Sept. 1, '62,	Killed at Fredericksburg, Va., December 13, 1862.
Smith, Peter	do	Sept. 1, '62,	Killed at Gettysburg, Pa., July 1, 1863.
Smith, Nicholas	do	Aug. 30, '62,	Killed at Fredericksburg, Va., Dec. 13, 1862—burial record, died at Richmond, December 31, 1862.
Sheets, Levi	do	Sept. 1, '62,	Deserted January 1, 1863.
Tompkins, Caleb	do	Sept. 1, '62,	Died at Washington, D. C., Feb. 7, 1863—buried in Military Asylum Cemetery.
Vanbuskirk, Wm	do	Aug. 30, '62,	Killed at Gettysburg, Pa., July 1, 1863—buried in National Cemetery, section B, grave 35.
Waters, Richard S.	do	Aug. 30, '62,	Disch. on Surg. cert., Jan. 19, 1863—re-enlisted March 30, 1864—tr. to 190th reg. P. V., May 29, 1865—Vet.
Weiscarrier, And.	do	Aug. 30, '62,	Killed at Gettysburg, Pa., July 1, 1863.
Wilson, Alex'r C.	do	Sept. 1, '62,	Deserted—date unknown.

APPENDIX.

DESCRIPTION

OF THE

BATTLE OF GETTYSBURG.

—

THIS description of the Battle of Gettysburg, and of General Lee's retreat from there, headed "The Valley of the Shadow of Death," I have taken from a small pamphlet which I purchased on the battle-field several years ago. I think it the most perfect description— as it actually occurred— I have ever read, and I am quite sure my comrades and friends will agree with me after they have perused it.

THE FIRST DAY.

JULY 1, 1863.

SUMMARY OF POINTS.—*First.* The battle begins on Seminary Ridge, about 9 A. M., with an engagement between Heth and Buford. *Second.* Engagement between the divisions of Heth and Pender of the Confederate Army and the First Corps of the Federal Army. *Third.* Death of General Reynolds. *Fourth.* Engagement between the divisions of Heth, Pender, Rodes and Early of the Confederate Army, and the First and Eleventh Corps of the Federal Army. *Fifth.* Repulse of the Federals, abandonment of Seminary Ridge, and occupation of Cemetery Hill; occupation of Gettysburg town by the Confederates. *Sixth.* Duration of the active fighting, a little less than seven hours.

A few minutes before nine o'clock on July 1st, Lieutenant-Colonel Kress, of General Wadsworth's staff, rode slowly into Gettysburg, ambling along on his chestnut charger, in no haste to accomplish his business, and avoiding the now active sun wherever the trees afforded a friendly shelter. Directing his horse to the nearest tavern, he found General Buford in front of the door, surrounded by his staff. The gallant cavalry general turned to him and said: "What are you doing here, sir?" Kress replied that he came to get some shoes for Wadsworth's division. Buford told him he had better return at once to his command. Kress said: "Why, what is the matter, general?" At that moment the far-off sound of a single gun—dull, prolonged, ominous—floated to them on the wings of the western breeze. Buford hastily mounted his horse, and, as he galloped off, answered the question of Kress: "*That's the matter!*" A few seconds later three cannon-shots were heard. Buford signals for his skirmishers to fire. They deliver a volley, and the battle of Gettysburg has begun.

Having satisfied himself the night before that he was about to be attacked, Buford was early in the saddle on this fateful day, placing the finishing touches upon his preparations to meet the foe. He had arranged his small force quite imposingly. Indeed, had he had at his command the half-million of troops that a farmer's wife, in reply to a Confederate officer's inquiry, declared were in Gettysburg, he could hardly have made a better showing. It was not only imposing, but it was far better—it was effective; for, when the Confederates attacked, "booming skirmishers, three deep," as Buford had predicted the night before, they met a stubborn and admirably-directed resistance.

His skirmish-line extended from the point where the Millerstown road crosses Willoughby Run, following the somewhat tortuous bluff bordering the left bank of that stream across the Chambersburg way, and thence around, crossing the Mummasburg, Carlisle, and Harrisburg pikes, and the railroad. On a ridge running parallel with Seminary Ridge, and half a mile from it, was posted the balance of his forces, dismounted. Covering the roads on which the enemy was first expected to advance, were planted the guns of his light batteries. It was with this disposition of his forces that the fight was opened.

Buford's men for the most part fought dismounted. This caused the Confederates to suppose them to be infantry, and, in consequence, Heth's division of Ewell's Corps, which precipitated the attack in an attempt to seize Gettysburg, moved tardily. A constantly increasing skirmish-fire was maintained for half an hour, when the artillery arrived to support Heth's men, and it at once opened with spirit. The guns of Buford made a prompt response, and were served with so much skill as to completely preserve the delusion that he was well supported. The fury of the fight increased every moment, and the gallant Buford was soon aware that the weight of numbers would shortly force him to fall back to Cemetery Hill, for which he had prepared. But not an inch did he yield ; hope told the flattering tale that reinforcements would soon be up. In his direst extremity, when every minute, every second counted, just as his heart sank the lowest, General Reynolds arrived, about a mile in advance of his corps. As soon as he had reconnoitred the field, he requested Buford to hold fast to his position, and said he would bring up the whole right wing of the army. He immediately sent dispatches in accord with this determination, and started to rejoin his now advancing men.

Cutler's brigade, of Wadsworth's division, led the advance of the supporting column. Three regiments of this brigade, the 76th and 147th New York, and the 56th Pennsylvania, went, under Wadsworth, to the right of the line, facing westward, north of the bed of the old unfinished railroad. The two remaining regiments, the 95th New York and the 14th Brooklyn, with Hall's Maine battery, Reynolds took to the south of the railroad grading, and placed them on a line with, but a little in advance of, the other regiments, the battery occupying the pike. As the infantry moved up, the cavalry retired. The regiments to the right of the cut had hardly reached their positions before they were heavily engaged. The force of men employed in exerting this pressure was the newly-placed regiments. They overlooked the west bank of Willoughby Run. Their artillery occupied the commanding points of the bluff.

While the attack on Cutler's brigade was in fierce progress, and the roar and rattle of musketry and cannon rose and fell like the irregular thunder of waves in a storm, General Doubleday arrived on the ground with the two remaining divisions of the First Corps. General Reynolds directed him to hold on to the road leading to Fairfield or Hagerstown, while he (General Reynolds) would maintain the possession of the Chambersburg pike.

There was a piece of woods between the two roads, triangular in shape, the base resting on Willoughby Run and the apex reaching up to Seminary Ridge, which seemed to Doubleday the key to the position. He made immediate arrangements to secure it, and not a moment too soon, as the enemy, appreciating the advantages of the spot, were already moving across Willoughby Run to attempt its possession. As the men filed past, Doubleday urged them to hold the woods at all hazards. Full of fight and enthusiasm, they replied to their commander : " If we can't hold it, where will you find the men who can ? " The answer was justified, for it was given by the men of the Iron Brigade, and they were commanded by Colonel

Morrow, of the 24th Michigan Volunteers. As the Iron Brigade went in on one side, Archer's brigade, preceded by a skirmish-line, went in on the other. Hardly had the two brigades locked horns in a discharge of their muskets, before the charge, led by the 2d Wisconsin, under Colonel Fairchild, swept suddenly and unexpectedly round the right flank of Archer's brigade, and captured a thousand prisoners, including Archer himself. The surprise of Archer's men was complete, for they supposed they were contending with militiamen hastily organized in the fright of the North at the actualities of invasion. When the Iron Brigade appeared, however, and Archer's men recognized their old antagonists, with the peculiar hats, a cry went up : "There are those damned black-hatted fellows again ! 'Tain't no militia. It's the Army of the Potomac."

Just as the Iron Brigade charged so gallantly, occurred one of the saddest incidents of that sad field—the death of General Reynolds. This great and gallant soldier was on his horse, at the edge of the woods, surrounded by his staff. Naturally anxious as to the result, he turned his head frequently to see if the troops were coming. While looking back in this way, one of the enemy's sharpshooters shot him in the head, the bullet entering the back of the head and coming out near the eye. He fell dead instantly and never spoke a word. It was a few minutes before 11 A. M. In the choice vigor of his full manhood, in the fullness of a well-earned military fame, perished this hero upon a field which his genius had fixed for the determination of one of the great and decisive conflicts of the world. Yet, as General Meade said, "where could man meet better the inevitable hour than in defense of his native State, his life-blood mingling with the soil on which he first drew breath?"

The death of Reynolds threw the command and the responsibility upon Doubleday. His first duty was to repair the damage inflicted on the right of his line, where Cutler's brigade had been driven back toward the town. The reserve, under Lieutenant-Colonel Dawes, with the assistance of Fowler's two regiments, accomplished the check of the enemy, drove a number of the enemy into the railroad cut, where they surrendered. This successful assault, while relieving Cutler's brigade from pursuit, also released the 147th New York, which, by the inroad of the Confederates, had been surrounded. It also enabled Doubleday's men to regain the gun lost by Hall's battery, and to reform the line where General Reynolds had placed it. The two regiments of Cutler's brigade were brought back from the town, and resumed the fighting with great gallantry.

There was now a lull in the combat. Heth was reorganizing his shattered front line, and Doubleday was waiting the arrival of more troops, pending the renewed onslaught. The Federals did not have long to wait. Pender's division, which had not yet been engaged, was now deployed, during which manœuvre the two remaining divisions of the First Corps, Rowley's and Robinson's, arrived on the field. The engagement was promptly renewed, and soon the courage and fighting character of the Bucktail brigade was offered the gage of proof. It was commanded by Colonel Stone, and fought with conspicuous bravery.

He was hardly in position before a new danger threatened. Ewell, with Stonewall Jackson's veterans, arrived. Deploying their skirmishers first on the Hunterstown road, they gradually pushed into every nook and corner where they could come unobserved on the Union line. Devin's brigade of cavalry faced them with determined signal courage. Never was a line of cavalry put to a severer strain. The ground whereon it stood was open, with no advantageous positions from which to fight. But taking advantage of every particle of fence, timber, or rise in front, the handful of Devin's men managed, with singular pluck, to temporarily arrest the progress of the veterans in gray.

General Howard arrived in advance of his corps, about 1 P. M., and, ranking General Doubleday, he assumed command. The latter took command of the First Corps, that of the Eleventh being turned over to Carl Schurz, who now had three divisions under him, commanded by Generals Von Steinwehr, Barlow, and Schimmelpfennig. Von Steinwehr promptly occupied Cemetery Hill with his division and the artillery, in accordance with an order of Reynolds. Barlow and Schimmelpfennig brought their men forward and relieved the gallant but sore-pressed men of Devin's brigade, who so valiantly were obstructing Ewell's march. Barlow extended his men round to the right as far as Rock Creek. Schimmelpfennig posted his to the left until they almost touched the right of the First Corps on Seminary Ridge.

The divisions of Pender and Heth were by this time developed to their full strength, and they faced the First Corps with nearly three times as many men as the Federals offered in opposition. Pender's left was extended so as to almost join Rode's division of Ewell's men. Some advantages of position compelled the Federals now to slightly alter their line of battle, but substantially they were defending an inner circle while the Confederates fought on an outer.

The fighting was most obstinate when it began, under these new arrangements, in a general advance of the Confederate infantry at 1.30 P. M. Opposed to the two corps of Federal troops—the First and Eleventh—were the divisions of Heth, Pender, Rodes, and Early, a full half of the Confederate army, with the remainder in supporting distance, or, in figures, 10,000 men opposed to 40,000. No wonder the fighting, if there was any, was obstinate; it had to be. For about two miles the Confederate formation was that of a "nearly continuous double line of deployed battalions, with other battalions in reserve." As it advanced it could not conform to the irregularity of the Union line, and in consequence the Confederate left became first engaged, striking the northern extrem'ty or right of the First Corps line. As there was a gap between the First and Eleventh Corps, Doubleday ordered Robinson, with all the reserve, Paul's and Baxter's brigades, assisted by Stewart's battery, of the 4th United States Artillery, to the weak spot, where, by desperate struggles, he was enabled to prevent the enemy from marching in.

By this time the battle was well under way. It was fierce, sanguinary, and determined. The Confederates fought with determined valor, and were resisted with more determination. Repeatedly the onslaughts against the old line—Stone, Wadsworth—and against Paul and Baxter were renewed, and as repeatedly thwarted. More daring leaders than the commanders of these brigades could not be found. Their men were of the same spirit, and, though suffering at every attack, they yet hurled back the foe and maintained their ground. The gallant Paul, in one of these, was paid for his bravery by a cruel wound, losing both his eyes.

While the chief force of the attack fell upon Robinson and Wadsworth, Stone was able to effectually supplement their operations; but when the enemy, unable to make an impression, turned upon Stone, Robinson and Wadsworth were too far away to return the compliment, and the blow fell with withering effect. In two lines, formed parallel to the pike, and at right angles to Wadsworth, the enemy first advanced upon Stone, who, anticipating such a movement, had thrown one of his regiments, under Colonel Dwight, forward to the railroad cut, where the men awaited the approach. When arrived at a fence, within pistol-shot, Dwight delivered a withering fire. Nothing daunted, the hostile lines crossed the fence, and continued to move forward. By this time Dwight's men had reloaded, and, when the advancing foe had arrived close upon the bank, they delivered another telling volley. They then leaped the bank and vaulted forward with the bayonet, uttering wild shouts, before which the foe fled in dismay. On returning, Dwight found that the enemy had planted a battery away to the west, so as to completely enfilade the railroad cut, making it untenable; whereupon he returned to his original position on the pike.

At this juncture Colonel Stone fell, severely wounded, and was borne off, the command devolving upon Colonel Wister. Foiled in their first attempt, with fresh troops the Confederate leaders came on from the northwest, that if possible the weak spot in the Bucktail line might be found. But Wister, disposing the regiment which in part faced the north to meet them, checked and drove them back from this point also. Again, with an enthusiasm never bated, they advanced from the north, and now crossing the railroad cut, which their guns guarded, rushed forward; but a resolute bayonet-charge sent them back again, and that front was once more clear. Believing that a single thin line, unsupported, unrenewed, and unprotected by breastworks, must eventually yield, a determined attack was again made from the west, but with no better results than before, being met by Colonel Huidekoper, who had succeeded to the command of Wister's regiment, and, though receiving a grievous wound, from the effect of which he lost his right arm, he held his ground, and the enemy retired once more in dismay.

The wave of battle as it rolled southward, reached every part in turn, and the extreme Union left, where Colonel Chapman Biddle's brigade was posted, at length felt its power. A body of troops, apparently an entire division, drawn out in heavy lines, came down from the west and south, and, overlapping both of Biddle's flanks, moved defiantly on. Only three small regiments were in position to receive them; but, ordering up the 151st Pennsylvania, and throwing it into the gap between Meredith's and his own, and wheeling the battery into position, Biddle awaited the approach. As the enemy appeared beyond the wood, under cover of which they had formed, a torrent of death-dealing missiles leaped from the guns. Terrible rents were made; but, closing up, they came on undaunted. Never were guns better served; and, though the ground was strewn with the slain, their line seemed instantly to grow together, as a stone thrown into the waves disappears and the waves flow together again. The infantry fire was terrific on both sides; but the enemy, outflanking Biddle, sent a direct and doubly destructive oblique fire, before which it seemed impossible to stand. But, though the dead fell until the living could fight from behind them as from a bulwark, the living stood fast, as if rooted to the ground.

While the battle was raging with such fury on the First Corps front, it was warmly maintained on the right, where two divisions of the Eleventh Corps had been posted. When General Howard first arrived on the field, and became aware that the enemy was advancing in great force from the north, he saw at a glance that Seminary Ridge would not for a moment be tenable unless the descent from this direction could be checked. Ewell, who was upon that front, seemed indisposed to make a determined assault until the bulk of his corps was up, and he could act in conjunction with the forces of Hill, advancing from the west. He accordingly pushed Rodes, with the advance division, over upon the right, until it formed a junction with Hill. He likewise sent the division of Early upon the left until he flanked the position which the cavalry of Buford was holding.

While Ewell was waiting, there was one labor being executed which proved of vital importance in the final cast of the battle: it was the fortifying of Cemetery Hill by Von Steinwehr. Around the base of this hill were low stone walls, tier above tier, extending from the Taneytown road around to the westerly extremity of Wolf's Hill. These afforded excellent protection to infantry, and behind them the soldiers, weary with the long march and covered with dust, threw themselves for rest. Upon the summit were beautiful green fields, now covered by second growth, which to the tread had the seeming of a carpet of velvet.

Von Steinwehr was an accomplished soldier, having been thoroughly schooled in the practice of the Prussian army. His military eye was delighted with this position, and thither he drew his heavy pieces, and planted them on the very summit, at the uttermost verge towards the town. But the position, though bold and commanding, was itself commanded, and Steinwehr instantly realized that there would be blows to take as well as to give. No tree, no house, no obstruction of any kind, shielded it from the innumerable points on the opposite hills, from Benner's, on the extreme right, beyond Wolf's Hill, around far south on Seminary Ridge to the left; but it stood out in bold relief, the guns presenting excellent targets for the enemy's missiles the moment he should come within artillery-range.

However powerful and effective his own guns might prove while unassailed, Steinwehr saw that they would be unable to live long when attacked, unless protected. Nor would any light works be of avail. There was no time to build a fort, for which the ground was admirably adapted. He accordingly threw up lunettes around each gun. These were not mere heaps of stubble and turf, but solid works of such height and thickness as to defy the most powerful bolts which the enemy could throw against them, with smooth and perfectly level platforms on which the guns could be worked. If the First and Eleventh Corps performed no other service in holding on to their positions, though sustaining fearful losses, the giving opportunity for the construction of these lunettes and getting a firm foothold upon this great vantage-ground, was ample compensation for every hardship and misfortune, and the labor and skill of Steinwehr in constructing them must ever remain a subject of admiration.

When Barlow, who commanded the division of the Eleventh Corps which took the right of line in front of the town, was going into position, he discovered a wooded eminence a little to the north of the point where the Harrisburg road crosses Rock Creek, and here he determined to made his right rest. It was the ground which the skirmish-line of Devin had held. But, as the cavalry retired, the enemy had immediately thrown forward a body of skirmishers to occupy it. To dislodge these, Barlow sent forward Von Gilsa's brigade. At the Almshouse the line halted, and knapsacks were thrown aside. It was then ordered to advance at double-quick. The order was gallantly executed, and the wood quickly cleared. Dispositions were made to hold it, and Wilkeson's battery, of the 4th United States, was advanced to its aid. The watchful Von Gilsa, however, soon discovered that the enemy was massed upon his flank, the brigades of Gordon and Hays, of Early's division, being formed under cover of the wooded ground on either side of Rock Creek, and ready to advance upon him. He found it impossible to hold this advanced position, and was obliged to allow that wing to fall back to the neighborhood of the Almshouse.

On the left, in the direction of the First Corps right, the brigade of Colonel Von Arnsburg was placed, with Dilger's and Wheeler's batteries. The extreme left was occupied by the 74th Pennsylvania. This regiment was much reduced in numbers, and in attempting to cover a long space it could present little more than a skirmish-line, which rested at a fence by a cross-road connecting the Carlisle and the Mummasburg ways. The Eleventh Corps line had hardly been established before the enemy, whose dispositions had been mainly perfected previous to its arrival, came down upon it with overwhelming might.

On the southern slope of Seminary Ridge, on a prolongation of the First Corps line northward, was a commanding position which the enemy could not be prevented from occupying, and where he now planted his artillery so as to send an oblique and very destructive fire upon the left of the Eleventh Corps. From this point also, having massed his infantry, he came on, sweeping past the right of the First Corps, and breaking and crumpling the left of the Eleventh. The right of the First, being thus turned, was obliged to retire, and was carried back. At this juncture Early, who was already massed on the extreme right flank of the Eleventh, also advanced. Near the Almshouse he met a stubborn resistance, and in the midst of the fight the gallant Barlow was wounded, and fell helpless into the enemy's hands. Stands were made at intervals, and the enemy held in check ; but it was impossible to stay the onset. Until the town was reached, the retirement was comparatively deliberate and orderly ; but when arrived there, being huddled in the narrow streets, subjected to a rapid fire from the batteries which raked them, and the enemy's swarming infantry intent on their destruction or capture, the men fell into confusion. Their officers strove to save them by ordering them into the cross-alleys. But this only added to the confusion, the men either not understanding the commands or hoping to escape the fire of the foe, and over twelve hundred were made prisoners in less than twenty minutes.

While this was passing upon the right, the enemy assaulted upon the left with no less vigor, but not with the same success. Though the First Corps had now been five hours in the fight, some portions of it six, and without supports or reliefs, it still stood fast, determined to make good the cry which they at the first had raised : " We have come to stay." But when it was known that the right of the corps had been turned, and that the Eleventh Corps was falling back, it became evident that the position which had been so long and so gallantly held, and withal with such substantial fruits, would have to be given up. Baxter's brigade, which had fought with stubborn bravery upon the right, was brought to the rear of the ridge at the railroad cut, where it defended a battery, and still held the enemy advancing from the north in check. Paul's brigade, having lost its commander, in retiring became entangled, and a considerable number fell into the enemy's hands. On the left, Meredith's and Biddle's brigades were ordered to fall back and cover the retirement of the balance of the line. Wister, who had succeeded to the command of Stone's brigade upon the fall of the latter, had likewise received a severe wound, and had turned over the brigade to Colonel Dana. At a barricade of rails which had been thrown up early in the day by Robinson's men, a final stand was made, and here the chief of artillery, Colonel Wainright, had posted his batteries, those of Cooper, Breck, Stevens, and Wilber, thus concentrating twelve guns in so small a space that they were scarcely five yards apart. Captain Stewart's battery was also in position on the summit, two pieces on either side of the railroad cut.

Encouraged by this falling back, the enemy was brought up in masses, as to an easy victory, and, forming in two lines, swept forward. As they approached, the artillery opened upon them. Stewart's guns being so far to right and front that he could enfilade their lines. Their front line was, by this concentrated fire, much broken and dispirited, but the second, which was also supported, pressed on. When arrived within musket-range their advance was checked, and the firing for a short time was hot. The rebels, who greatly outnumbered the small Union line, now began to show themselves upon the left flank. Seeing that the position could not much longer be held, Doubleday ordered the artillery to retire, and it moved in good order from the field, wending its way back to Cemetery Hill. But, before the pieces were all away, the enemy had gained so far upon the flank as to reach it with his musketry-fire, shielding himself behind a garden-fence which runs within fifty yards of the pike. Before the last piece had passed, the fire had become very warm, and the horses attached to this gun were shot. The piece, consequently, had to be abandoned, together with three caissons.

The infantry held its position behind the barricade, successfully checking the enemy in front, the men showing the most unflinching determination, Captain Richardson, of General Meredith's staff, riding up and down the line waving a regimental flag, and encouraging them to duty. But the enemy was now swarming upon the very summit of the ridge, upon the left flank of Doubleday. So near had they approached, that Lieutenant-Colonel McFarland, while reconnoitring to discover their exact position, received a volley which shattered both legs. "When all the troops at this point," says General Doubleday, "were overpowered, Captain Glenn, of the 149th Pennsylvania, in command of the Headquarter Guard, defended the building [Seminary] for full twenty minutes against a whole brigade of the enemy, enabling the few remaining troops, the ambulances, and artillery, to retreat in comparative safety."

And now was seen the great advantage in the position of Steinwehr's reserves. As the begrimed cannoneers, and the beasts foaming with the excitement of battle, and the sadly-thinned ranks of infantry, exhausted by six hours of continuous fighting, filed through the town and approached Cemetery Hill, they came as to the folds of an impregnable fortress. Here at length was rest and security. Whenever the foeman attempted to follow, they came immediately into range of Steinwehr's well-posted guns, and at every stone wall and building was an abattis of bayonets. The heroic Buford, who had first felt the shock of battle, and during the long hours of this terrible day had held his troops upon the flanks of the infantry, joining in the fierce fighting as opportunity or necessity required, and who from his watch-tower had scanned and reported every phase of the battle, was now at the critical moment a pillar of strength. The insignificant division of Steinwehr would alone have presented but a narrow barrier to a powerful and triumphant foe, intent on pushing his advantage, and to the left, where country is all open, and nature presents no impediment to an advance, it could have been flanked and easily turned out of its position. But here, like a wall of adamant, stood the veterans of Buford, with guns skillfully posted, ready to dispute the progress of the enemy. His front was tried, and the attempt was made to push past him along the low ground drained by Stevens Run, where some severe fighting occurred. But he maintained his ground intact, and that admirable position was again saved.

On the right of Steinwehr's position were the rugged heights of Wolf's Hill, a natural buttress, unassailable in front from its abruptness, and, though susceptible of being turned, as it was on the following evening, yet so curtained by an impenetrable wood as to convey the suspicion of danger lurking therein. Early, who was in front of this hill, made some attempts to carry it, but, finding it apparently well protected, did not push his reconnoisance.

As the two broken corps of the Union army ascended Cemetery Hill, they were met by staff officers, who turned the Eleventh Corps to the right and the First Corps to the left, where they went into position along the summit of the ridge stretching out on either hand from the Baltimore pike. A ravine to the right of Cemetery Hill, and between that and Wolf's Hill, seemed to present to the enemy a favorable point of attack, and hither was at once sent

Stevens's Maine battery and Wadsworth's division of the First Corps. Here Wadsworth immediately commenced substantial breastworks along the brow of the hill, an example which other troops followed, until the whole front, extending to Spangler's Spring, was surmounted by one of like strength. Through that ravine the enemy did assail, but the preparations to meet him were too thorough to admit of his entrance.

This ended the first day of the great conflict. The combatants drew breath, and under cover of the now rapidly falling night, rested: the soldiers upon the earth anywhere, the officers in earnest thought for the morrow, when again would be upreared the purple banners of horrid war.

The results of the first day may be thus summed up: In the face of the most disastrous odds, the Federal troops that were engaged held the ground on which the battle opened, and finally surrendered it only in the face of the whole Confederate army; the Union army ended the day much dispirited, driven from their position, and disorganized by a panic to which was added the disheartening influence of the death of Reynolds, undoubtedly the most remarkable man among all the officers that the Army of the Potomac saw fall in battle during the four years of its existence; the Confederates were in high spirits over the substantial advantages they had gained, and went into bivouac with eager desire for daylight and the renewal of the contest.

THE SECOND DAY.

July 2, 1863.

SUMMARY OF POINTS.—Federal positions arranged and occupied. Skirmishing by various small commands. Battle begun at 3.30 P. M. Attack on Federal left, commanded by Sickles, by First Confederate Corps, commanded by Longstreet. The severe engagements of the Peach Orchard, Devil's Den, and Wheat Field. Vincent's occupation and defense of Little Round Top. Final Repulse of Longstreet's assaults, and cessation of fighting on Federal left, 8 P. M. Ewell's attack on Culp's Hill begins at 5 P. M. Johnson on extreme Federal left. Early on Cemetery Hill. Charge of the Louisiana Tigers. Repulse of Confederates, and cessation of fighting on Federal right, 9 P. M. Duration of battle, four hours and a half on Federal left, four hours on Federal right.

Everyone felt that the dawn of the second of July would herald the critical hour of the conflict. The hot breathless night that was hastening to a close when Meade arrived on the field seemed to augur the approach of death, and presage the inevitable slaughter of the day now breaking. What thoughts must have been his! Holding supreme command less than a week, and already engaged in a battle in which was enveloped the fate of the Republic!

When he reached the battle-field, at 1 A. M. of this day, he found the Eleventh Corps occupying Cemetery Hill, along which had rallied Schurz's division across the Baltimore road; Steinwehr's on the left, and on the right and rear Barlow's men, now commanded by Ames. The First Corps was divided: Wadsworth, on the right of Ames, held Culp's Hill; Robinson, on the left of Steinwehr and across the Taneytown road, extended as far as a clump of trees called Ziegler's Grove; Doubleday, who had transferred the command of the corps to General Newton, was in reserve with his division in the rear of Schurz. The combined artillery of these two corps covered their front, sheltered to a great extent by the light earth-works constructed on Cemetery Hill the previous day. South of Ziegler's Grove, Hancock had, since the evening of the 1st, prolonged the Federal left, with the troops he had at his disposal, as far as the Round Tops, so as to present a solid line to the enemy's troops, which he then perceived on Seminary Ridge. Birney, with Graham's and Ward's brigades of the Third Corps bearing to the left of Robinson, extended along the ridge which prolongs Cemetery Hill as far as the depression where the latter seems to lose itself for awhile, to rise again afterwards toward the Round Tops. Williams, with the other divisions of the same corps, had halted within a mile and a quarter in the rear of Cemetery Hill, on the left bank of Rock Creek, near the point where the Baltimore road crosses this stream. Finally, Humphreys, who had not had time in daylight to choose a position, massed his two brigades a little to the rear and to the left of Birney's line. Meade, as soon as he saw the ground by daylight, saw that it possessed several weak spots; but, being too late to withdraw, he hastened to strengthen everything by hurrying forward all the troops not yet at Gettysburg. By forced marches the whole army reached him by 9 A. M., with the exception of fifteen thousand men of the Sixth Corps, who were distant but a few hours.

Lee's positions at daybreak on the 2d were as follows: Ewell's entire corps was drawn up on the battle-field, with Johnson on the left, resting on Rock Creek, upon Benner's Hill; Early in the center, facing the ridge which connects Culp's Hill with Cemetery Hill;

Rodes on the right, at the foot of Cemetery Hill, his main force occupying the town of Gettysburg, while his right formed a connection with the Third Corps on Seminary Ridge. The two divisions of the Third, those of Heth and Pender, retained the positions they had taken at sunset on the day previous. Pender was on the left, above the Seminary; Heth on the right, along the ridge; Hill's third division, under Anderson, was posted about one and a half miles in the rear, on the Cashtown road, between Marsh Creek and Willoughby Run. By 4 A. M., Anderson was on his way to Seminary Ridge, closely followed by McLaw's and Hood's divisions— with the exception of Law's brigade—of the First Corps. At the same time, Pickett was leaving Chambersburg; Laws, the village of New Guilford; and Stuart, Carlisle. By 9 A. M., therefore, the entire Confederate army enveloped Gettysburg, with the exception of Stuart's cavalry and the six thousand men of Laws and Pickett.

Meade, on examining the ground, issued his orders, and rectified his positions, and placed the constantly-arriving troops in position, all of which was accomplished by 9 A. M. During the five hours up to this time, the enemy had not fired a shot or annoyed the Union commander at all. Nor did he do so until much more precious time had been wasted in the most extraordinary fashion: for time was everything to the Confederate chieftain. He decided early on the 2d to attack the Federal left, and to intrust the command to Longstreet. The sound of the battle is to be the signal for an attack on the Federal left by Ewell, and, if success seems to favor these attacks, the center, under Hill, is to attack the center of Meade's line. This plan makes success dependent upon the combined action of several corps between which there is absolutely no connection, a plan that has failed so often as to have almost become a dead law of battle.

The sun by this time has crossed the zenith, and the same strange ominous silence broods over the fields separating the two armies. Meade is more and more astonished at Lee's inaction. The signal-men on Round Top signal Meade that Confederate troops are moving to the south. All morning skirmishing, more or less severe, has been going on on Meade's left, and he is now assured that the attack will be there. This is the view taken by Sickles, who, considering that his instructions have not been definite, undertakes, on his own responsibility, to push forward and occupy the Emmettsburg road, possessing himself of Sherfy's peach-orchard. The position was appreciated by Lee, and Longstreet's first purpose was to obtain it. Meade, on reaching the ground, saw at once that it could not be held by the troops then present, and hastened for reinforcements. It was, however, too late to fall back. The Confederate artillery were pouring shot and shell into the orchard, and, a little more to the east, the rattle of musketry disclosed the fact that Hood had opened the fight.

For some time the fire of the artillery was tremendous. It proved but the introduction to more deadly work. Longstreet had formed his lines under cover, and was now moving down to strike the extreme left of Meade's line. With a wild charge they confronted the troops of Ward, who were enabled to beat them back. But Ward realized at once that he could not withstand a second assault. De Trobriand, therefore, at his request, sent him the 17th Maine, which took position behind a low stone wall to the left of the wheat-field, where it could do effective work if Ward should be forced back. The 17th Maine was followed by the 40th New York, which took position on Ward's left, so as to block the way to Little Round Top. The attack was not again directed against Ward, but against the whole of Birney's line, reaching forward to the orchard. De Trobriand's men were assaulted with murderous fire and desperate courage. The troops of Graham, which were on open ground and had no protection, were in imminent danger of being cut to pieces. The cut where the road-bed makes up to the Emmettsburg way afforded a slight protection from artillery-fire, but was of no avail when the Confederate infantry charged. The 141st Pennsylvania was posted in support of the Federal guns at this point, facing south. The men were lying down when the charge came, and were unperceived by the foe, which swept forward to seize the guns. Suddenly the men of the 141st rose, poured in a well-directed volley, and followed the smoke of their guns with a wild bayonet-charge. Swept down by ranks, and bewildered by the suddenness of the unexpected regiment, the Confederate line halted, paused, trembled and fled. The horses of the Union artillery having all been killed, the guns were drawn back by the infantry to the rear of the road-bed.

While this wave of battle, extending from the Round Top west to the orchard, was rolled again and again at the devoted line of blue-coats, Hood, who had instantly appreciated the value of Round Top on seeing it, was organizing a movement to attempt its capture. He had discovered that Little Round Top was not occupied, and that only a thin curtain, composed of the 99th Pennsylvania, was hung in front of the hill. This place he regarded as the prize of the day. Selecting his most trusted men for the assault, he led them out and pointed to the dark ground of the rocky summit which he desired them to possess. On they rushed with wild impetuosity; but, before they could reach the thin line of the 99th, succor had come. The 40th New York, the 6th New Jersey, and the 4th Massachusetts arrived and occupied the path across Plum Run. With desperate valor the enemy penetrate the Union line, and, with still further impetuosity, rush on to the foot of the mountain-side. Suddenly a sheet of flame bursts in their astonished faces. The hill, ten minutes ago unoccupied, swarms at its base with the men of Vincent's brigade, ordered to Little Round Top by Sykes, at the request of General Warren, who has appreciated to the full the importance of this hill. In addition, Warren, hastening to some troops he sees moving close by, finds them to be the third brigade of Ayres's division of the Fifth Corps, under General Weed. The first regiment Warren encounters is commanded by an old friend, Colonel O'Rorke, who, in answer to Warren's demands, causes the column of the 140th New York to directly scale the acclivities of Little Round Top. This the men do willingly.

All the while Laws's soldiers are pressing Vincent, who defends his position at the point of the muzzle. It is almost hand to hand. Laws, seeing the resistance offered by this small band, determines to end it by a flank movement, at the expense of the 16th Michigan. Extending his left, he attacks with impetuosity, and carries his point. The 16th is unable to resist, gives way, Vincent is cut off from the rest of the army, and cannot, therefore, protect the point of the position—the summit of Little Round Top—on which the officers of the Signal Corps are still waving their colors. At the very moment the 16th Michigan gives way and Laws's men break for the summit, O'Rorke's soldiers reach the top at full run, which Warren has pointed out to them as a citadel to be held at all odds. Not a moment too soon do they arrive. There is no time to contemplate the battle-field below, which is enveloped in a pall of sulphurous smoke. Laws's soldiers are just appearing on the other side. There is no time to form a line, load their guns, or fix bayonets. O'Rorke, seizing the position in a glance, calls on his willing men. The enemy fires: a large number of the 140th fall on the soil they have never seen, but so well won. With a wild scream, the rest, clubbing their muskets and raising them on high, dash down upon those who a moment since deemed themselves victors.

The Confederate advance is checked; the prize seems lost. The foremost of Laws's men are taken prisoners, and a terrible fire is opened on the remainder. Vincent's right, having recovered from its check, now dashes forward once more. Hazlett's battery, which, after the most extraordinary exertions on the part of the men of the 140th New York, has been hauled to the summit, now takes position, though menaced by showers of bullets. The guns cannot be depressed enough to do damage to the enemy on the immediate slope below their muzzles, and they are therefore trained on the Confederate reserve in the valley, and the sound of the guns encourages the Union infantry. The valiant O'Rorke has unhappily fallen; the 140th has lost over one hundred men in a few minutes; the battle waxes more and more intense. Another attempt to pierce the line is made by Laws, but Vincent hastens there with a few reinforcements, and the attempt is defeated. Vincent falls a victim to his bravery, Hood is severely wounded, and the combatants, somewhat exhausted, pause for breath.

On the other side of Plum Run, at this time, the Union positions so stubbornly defended by Ward and De Trobriand are seriously compromised by the arrival of Kershaw, who forces Barnes off the ground he is holding. Ward is obliged to abandon the entire hill of the Devil's Den. The Confederates, crowding the wood, take the 17th Maine, posted behind the wall, in flank, and, rushing across to the wheat-field, force Winslow's guns to the rear, and menace De Trobriand's weak line. De Trobriand is at the same time assailed in front by Anderson's men, and is compelled to give way. The troops in the orchard on his right cannot give him any assistance, for the artillery which they are there to defend is now threatened by Kershaw's left. The 8th South Carolina makes a valiant attempt to capture the guns of Clark and Bigelow, but are stopped by an appalling fire from the 141st Pennsylvania, who suddenly rise from a sunken road. Under cover of this success, the guns are hauled back beyond the position of peril. This further uncovers De Trobriand's right. Caldwell's strong division now arrives, in time to relieve Birney and Barnes. One brigade, under Cross, advances to De Trobriand's support; a second, under Kelly, which has crossed Plum Run near the road, supports Ward along the slopes bordering this stream a little lower down. This is Meagher's Irish brigade, and they go into the fight in characteristic fashion. When within range of the enemy, the command is halted, the men kneel, and their chaplain, a priest of Rome, standing on a high rock, a natural pulpit, pronounces a general absolution. The "Amen" of the priest is simultaneous with Kelly's "Forward!" and, with the Church's benediction, these brave fellows rush onward. Their onslaught stays the advance of Anderson's brigade. The priest and the soldier together have been irresistible.

In the meantime, Birney, rallying around Cross a portion of De Trobriand's soldiers and Burling's two regiments, which have been driven in on that side, calls on them to follow him, and a dash is made at Kershaw's line, which cannot resist this assault, and is forced back on Somms's brigade, a hundred and fifty yards to the rear. These troops advance against Caldwell's first line, which, losing heavily, is supplanted by the second, composed of the brigades of Zook and Brooke. These men drive Somms to the other side of the ravine. Kershaw, on the left, is likewise dislodged by the fury of Caldwell's attack, and the Confederates find it necessary to retire, as it were, for breath to renew the struggle. Hood is now exhausted, and McLaws, seeing that Somms and Kershaw are unable to hold their ground, decides to direct the main attack on the orchard. Sickles has given Graham the effectives of two brigades to defend it, but it would require strong intrenchments to cover so destitute a position. The Confederate artillery-fire is slackened; the infantry, under Barksdale of Mississippi, strikes Graham's flank that faces westward. Woffard, with some of Kershaw's battalions, leaps upon Graham from the south, and the devoted Union commander passes through a vortex of fire to find himself wounded and a prisoner. His soldiers are prisoners or dispersed. The orchard is captured after a prolonged and gallant defense. The batteries along the Emmettsburg road are withdrawn: it is no longer possible to maintain them. Those on the left are being fired as they are withdrawn. They crowd forward. Birney is defeated: more than half his men are lost. Barksdale pushes on to the front. Woffard bears to the eastward, in order to take in flank the regiments that hold Kershaw in check. Anderson's three brigades, under Wilcox, Perry and Wright, hasten to dislodge Humphreys from his position on the Emmettsburg road. It is about a quarter to seven. Humphreys's left is turned, and, ordered by Birney, he executes a masterly movement to the rear, reforming his line of battle under the most difficult circumstances. By this time, Barnes and Caldwell are finally driven out of the wheat-field. Zook is killed on this bloody ground. The Federal line is irrevocably broken, and all the forces which till then have held Longstreet in check are no longer able to reform it. A gradual concentration and falling back on Little Round Top, the real point of support for the Federal left, now takes place. It was inevitable.

Let us now return to this splendid position, which we left on the temporary cessation of the Confederate attack. Weed's brigade has been ordered by Sykes to reinforce the 140th New York, and has promptly complied. Weed reaches there at the moment Vincent falls mortally wounded, and when both sides are preparing to renew the fight. Laws makes a determined onslaught on the 20th Maine, and a hand-to-hand fight ensues. Weed sets an example of heroic bravery, and falls mortally wounded by the side of Hazlett's battery. Hazlett, bending down to receive the dying man's last words, is also struck, and falls lifeless upon the body of his chief. The carnage is fearful. Happily the enemy is nearly exhausted, and, in his attempt to surround the left of the Federals, he has prolonged his line too much. Colonel Chamberlain takes advantage of it to charge the enemy in turn, which so surprises the Confederates that they fall back in dismay, leaving more than three hundred wounded and prisoners. The brigades of General Ayres on Plum Run, and the arrival of Crawford with McCandless's brigade on Little Round Top, suffice to drive the enemy over Plum Run, with which movement ceases the struggle for the possession of this vantage-ground. It has been bitter, costly, desperate and triumphant for its defenders.

The battle continues for the possession of the hills in and about Plum Run. Barksdale and Woffard attack Humphreys's weak division, and Hancock—who took command on the retirement of Sickles—hurries to the support of Humphreys all the forces at his disposal. Two regiments of Hays's division, Willard's brigade, and thirty or forty pieces of reserve artillery under Major McGilvery, accomplish the immediate support, while Meade, summoning from the right, sends Williams's division, closely followed by one of Geary's brigades, under Candy, and preceded by Lockwood's two regiments, to the front. Three other brigades are also hurried forward, and Meade calls upon General Newton to weaken Cemetery Hill as much as possible, in order to assist Humphreys. The final assault of the Confederates on the Union left now takes place, and is led by Anderson, McLaws, Wilcox and Barksdale, Longstreet directing in person. Hood could not advance, owing to the possession of Plumb Run and Little Round Top by the Federals. These are ready to receive them, and have now occupied Big Round Top also, thus closing all access on that end. The fight becomes furious. The fiery Barksdale is shot, under the fire of Burling's regiment. His soldiers, carried away by his bravery, rush upon the Federals, but are thrown back in disorder, leaving their dying chief in the hands of the Unionists. Woffard, who is supporting Barksdale on the right, cannot go beyond the flats of Plum Run; Anderson's brigade, on the left, is not within reach. Longstreet waits in vain for Somms and Kershaw, whose brigades have suffered too much, and cannot renew the attack. At this moment Anderson's division scales the slopes along which Humphreys and Gibbon are posted. Wilcox, on the right, followed at a considerable distance by Perry, leads the attack. On the left, Wright, receiving the oblique fire of several guns posted on the edge of a small wood above Gibbon's front, rushes forward and captures them; but Webb's brigade, emerging from its position, makes a desperate stand in defense of the hill. Wright, encouraged by the sight of the crowds that are encumbering the Baltimore road, believes he is about to become the master of the hill, and fights with sublime fury. In fifteen minutes he loses two-thirds of his effective force, and is compelled to fall back before Gibbon's division, which is facing him with ideal courage. Wilcox, taken in flank by McGilvery's artillery, instead of the retreating soldiers he supposed he was pursuing, comes suddenly upon Humphreys's (in good order) and Hancock's reserves, and into a circle of fire which in a breath strips from him five hundred men of the sixteen hundred with him. Dispirited, broken, sullen, he retires to the Emmettsburg road. The last effort against the Federals has failed; and, as the twilight creeps in to cover the scene of blood and death, the musketry-fire ceases, the artillery languishes, and the pall of smoke drifts away on the rising night-breeze. The agony here is over.

During most of this time, Ewell, commanding the Confederate left, has been waiting the sound of Longstreet's guns to convey to him the order for attack. A contrary wind prevailing, he does not hear the sounds of battle until five o'clock. Then he prepares at once. Six batteries on Benner's Hill open fire in support of the attack of Johnson's division on the Federal positions on Culp's Hill. An hour suffices to silence the fire of these guns, so well is the Federal artillery served. Finding an attempt on the north and northeast sides of Culp's Hill impossible, Johnson determines to attack the Federals in the very gorges of Rock Creek, in order to turn their positions by way of the southeast. About half-past six he is in position and opens fire, and for the first time on the 2d of July the battle is in progress along the whole front of both armies.

While Johnson was pushing in the right of the line on Culp's Hill, those who defended Cemetery Hill were about to face the first historic charge of the battle—that of the Louisiana Tigers. The summit of Cemetery Hill was held by Weidrick's and Rickett's batteries, supported by a part of the Eleventh Corps, under cover of stone walls. To the right of Cemetery Hill, at right angles to it, was the beginning of Culp's Hill, upon a small plateau of which was planted Stevens's Maine battery. His guns enfiladed the approaches to Cemetery Hill. On the right of Stevens's battery began the heavy breastworks erected by Wadsworth on the top of Culp's Hill, and overhanging its precipitous sides. This earth-work was carried round the hill, and was continued by Greene, whose right rested at a ravine that declines to a thickly-wooded plateau. These breastworks were continued beyond the ravine, but at this hour had no infantry to make them effective, the troops having been ordered to Round Top.

Just as the sun was disappearing in the red west and the soft gray shadows of twilight were gathering like a ghostly army, the defenders of Cemetery Hill saw emerging from behind an eminence near the town a long line of infantry formed for assault. Onward the column moved with the precision of a parade and all the steadiness of a holiday spectacle. The line was formed of the brigades of Hays and Hoke, led by the famous Louisiana Tigers. The moment they came in sight, they faced the test of death. Stevens opened on them with every gun: Weidrick and Ricketts joined in the chorus. The slaughter was immediately terrible; men fell dead before the iron storm at the rate of a dozen a minute. The guns of Ricketts were charged with canister, and they fired every fifteen seconds. Stevens's battery, enfilading the Confederate line, wreaked furious destruction upon the storming column, which, through it all, in the face of the very hell of war, kept on their upward way. As the Tigers came within musket-range of the crest of Cemetery Hill, Howard's infantry, hidden behind the stone wall, poured volley after volley into the faces of the wild-hearted and maddened men. But the eyes of two armies were on the Tigers; they carried the guerdon of fame that they had never failed in a charge. They could not halt now, the hour of their hardest trial. Over the stone walls they went at a bound. Stevens was obliged to cease firing, for fear of killing friends. Weidrick is unable to withstand the shock; his supports and his men are swept back together before the force of that human tornado. Ricketts quails not; the full strength of the storm, falling on his devoted men, falls in vain. His left piece is taken: the Tigers are within the cage. The remaining guns are still served with admirable discipline and courage, drivers and officers taking the places of the dead cannoneers. A struggle takes place for the guidon; it is in the hands of a Tiger; Lieutenant Brockway seizes a stone, hurls it full at the head of the soldier, which fells him to the ground, and in a moment the Tiger is shot with his own musket. The wildest confusion—a bedlam of terror—now ensues. The rapidly-gathering darkness makes friends and foes indistinguishable. The men at the batteries are being overpowered by their desperate and maddened assailants, but still they cling to their guns; with hand-spikes, rammers and stones they defend their position, shouting to one another: "Death on our own State soil rather than give the enemy the guns!" The moment is most critical; the fate of the issue is near at hand. At this instant Carroll's brigade rushes in to the rescue; with wild shouts they burst upon the almost exhausted foe. They waver, they turn, they retreat in confusion. Ricketts's men fly to their guns, double-shot them, and fire deadly parting salutes at the defeated Tigers. Their charge is over; they have been beaten. Nearly twelve hundred of their seventeen hundred are left dead and dying. It has been indeed a bloody half-hour's work. They pass down the hill, out into the darkness, and are seen no more in history.

All the while Johnson is battling with persistent force against Greene on Culp's Hill. Unable to beat in his line defending the breastworks, he seizes the line thrown up by Ruger and Geary and abandoned when these commanders were ordered to reinforce the Federals on Plum Run. Again and again Johnson assails Greene, and again and again is he driven back with dismay. Finding it impossible to break down this gallant soldier, Johnson pushes on past Culp's Hill, and has almost reached the Baltimore pike when the now offensive darkness comes to the aid of the Federals, and Johnson halts his men. The battle of the second day is over, and in the deep shadows of welcome night the tired men throw themselves down, not caring whether the sod or a corpse is their pillow.

In the early hours of the night the leaders sum up the day's total. During the terrible storm, the Confederates have acquitted themselves with the courage and ardor that have so frequently secured victory to them. Nevertheless, they have not achieved the results which they were entitled to expect from their enormous sacrifices. The condition of the battle-field has been against them, and in favor of the Union arms. Though defeated on the right, they have won such advantages on the left that Lee is more than justified in renewing the attack. The situation of Meade, in spite of the advantages he has gained, is properly alarming. His losses are enormous—more than twenty thousand for two days' fighting! The enemy has not spoken his best word, and the Union commander is fearful lest another day's conflict equally murderous would cause his army to melt away into nothing. A council of war decides to fight it out on the morrow, and the rest of the now moonlit night is occupied in preparations for the coming final and fierce whirlwind of strife that is to decide the battle and the life of the Republic.

THE THIRD DAY.

JULY 3, 1863.

SUMMARY OF POINTS.—3.40 A. M., Federal attack on Confederate left, on Culp's Hill. Final repulse and re-occupation of Culp's Hill positions, 11 A. M. Federal cavalry attack on Confederate trains on Confederate right. Sharp skirmishing 11 to 11.45 A. M. 1 P. M., artillery-duel begins. Pickett's charge, 2.30 P. M. Final repulse of Confederate attack about 3.15 P. M. Desultory fighting up to 6 P. M. Duration of fighting on Federal right, seven hours; on Federal left, about five hours.

The kindly moon lights up the battle-field all the night of the 2d–3d, as though it were desirous nothing should hinder the prompt resumption of hostilities. The wounded are cared for as far as possible, and the lines of both armies are rectified and strengthened. Lee intends to renew his attack on the Federal right, where Johnson has gained such an advantage, and attempt also to pierce the Union center. Meade determines to push Johnson back, and then to await developments. In addition to his reports from the battle-field, Meade is aware that Stuart and Kilpatrick have met, and fought a sharp engagement, which has, however, no bearing on the final conflict of both armies, now about to take place.

During the night, Geary's and Ruger's divisions were ordered back to Culp's Hill. Geary, finding his old ground occupied, formed on Greene's right. Ruger took position on the flank and rear of

Johnson's men. Shortly after 3 A. M., General Kane observed the enemy moving about, preparatory, presumably, to a charge. Reporting to Geary, that officer promptly took the offensive, and at twenty minutes before four, discharged his pistol as a signal for opening the attack. The conflict, thus begun, continued for seven hours with intense bitterness. The firing of the Union troops was most effective: the Confederate charges, which were made with great spirit, availed nothing. The artillery-fire from the Union lines was well directed, and accomplished much damage: the Confederate forces being unable to get their artillery into any position from which an effective reply could be made. As the day wears on, the sun beats upon the troops with unstinted fury, making the terrible situation more terrible still. The struggle is terrific: hand to hand, man to man, almost impossible to describe, as it is made up of incidents of bravery and accidents of death as numerous as the combatants themselves. A terrific charge by Stonewall Jackson's old command, made with useless heroism upon Kane's brigade of Geary's division, failing, Johnson was at last convinced—at 11 A. M. —that he could effect nothing further, and, to a return-charge of Geary's division, he yielded his ground slowly and reluctantly. With a yell of congratulation, Geary's men re-occupied their breastworks. This ended all attempts to turn the Federal right, and, beyond a fusilade now and again when anything showed itself, the Confederate forces of Ewell gave their opponents no further trouble.

The final scene is now to transpire before the eyes of the devoted men of both armies. One more terrific tableau and the battle is done. Lee will attempt to break the Federal center. He had failed to break the left—he had failed to turn the right. He must pierce the center, or retreat. For this purpose, he has Pickett's division—the flower of the grand old commonwealth of Virginia— which has not yet been in action, and which is full of enthusiasm. They will lead, they will follow, anywhere. He decides to launch them on the center, and to support them on both flanks by an advance of the balance of his available army. It will be a supreme effort—the last desperate chance of a desperate man. Longstreet's men, the soldiers under Hood and McLaws, have suffered too much to undertake the support of Pickett. They remain inactive spectators of Pickett's efforts. Lee therefore forms Pickett's division in two lines—Kemper and Garnett leading, supported by Armistead, with Wilcox and Perry, of Hill's Corps, on his right, and Pettigrew, commanding Heth's division, and Trimble, with two of Pender's brigades, of Hill's Corps, for a like purpose on his left. Pickett explains the purpose of the charge, and designates to each officer his exact position. Everything is ready to go forward, after the artillery has cleared the way. Longstreet does not approve of the assault. Lee overrules his objections; and the plan, as projected by the Confederate commander, is executed.

To the Confederate artillery is entrusted the heavy work. At daybreak, Colonel Alexander places the six reserve batteries of the First Corps along the Emmettsburg road; the rest of the artillery of this corps is presently posted in this vicinity, and both form a slightly concave line, of seventy-five pieces, from the peach-orchard to a point which commands the road east of the Godori house, at a distance of from nine hundred to thirteen hundred yards from the Federal line. The batteries of Major Henry, to the right of the orchard, cross their fire with that of the rest of the line. Alexander's batteries are ranged above this position, at the summit of the slope running down to the Trostle house. On his left, and somewhat in his rear, is located the Washington Artillery, with Dearing's and Cabell's battalions. To this line, Meade was not able to oppose as many guns, owing to the shorter space at his disposal. At Cemetery Hill, on the right, were the batteries of Ricketts, Wiedrick, Dilger, Bancroft, Eakin, Wheeler, Hill, and Taft, under command of Major Osborn. Next to him, and directly in front of Meade's headquarters, extending from Ziegler's Grove south along Hancock's front, were the batteries of Woodruff, Arnold, Cushing, Brown, and Rorty, commanded by Major Hazard. Still further on the Federal left was Major McGilvery, commanding the batteries of Thomas, Thompson, Phillips, Hart, Sterling, Roch, Cooper, Dow, and Ames. Gibbs and Rittenhouse held the summit of Little Round Top. Eighty guns were thus in effective position. The Union infantry supporting this artillery consists of Robinson's division of the First Corps, at Ziegler's Grove, and to his left the divisions of Hays and Gibbon, of the Second Corps, and that of Doubleday, of the First. To the left again were Caldwell, of the Second, and parts of the Third, Fifth and Sixth Corps.

By one o'clock, the enemy having perfected his arrangements, Longstreet reluctantly sends word to Colonel Walton to give signal. Two cannon-shots, fired on the right by the Washington Artillery at an interval of a minute, break the silence brooding over the scorched and waiting battle-field. The signal is well understood by both armies, and the solitary smoke of these shots has not dispersed before the whole Confederate line is ablaze. The throats of one hundred and thirty-eight cannon obey the signal, and send forth a concerted roar that rivals the angriest thunder. The Federal guns wait, under General Hunt's orders, fifteen minutes before replying, in order to take a survey of the batteries upon which they must concentrate their fire. Their positions afford better shelter than those of the enemy, but the formation of the Federal line affords the Confederates the advantages of a concentric fire. By 1.15 P. M., the reply is made. More than two hundred guns are now engaged in the most tremendous and most terrible artillery-duel ever witnessed in the New World. Every size and form of shell, known to British and American gunnery, shrieks, moans, whistles and wrathfully flutters over the ground. As many as six in a second—for the Confederate batteries fire volleys constantly twice in a second—bursting and screaming, carry destruction everywhere, and everywhere ruin and dismay. It is a hell of fire, that amazes the greatest veteran present. The wild death-screams of the shells are answered with the peculiar yells of the dying: the blent cry of pain, and horror and despair! It is an hour of terror. Death is master of the situation. The roar of the iron storm cannot drown the accordant shriek of the dying, the wild curse of the wounded, the avenging oaths of the living. Was there ever such a scene? The fire of the Federals is effective, but General Hunt, anticipating the infantry-attack soon to follow, orders a cessation, and the batteries on Cemetery Hill cease their angry answers. They are followed by the rest, and soon the Confederate guns hear no reply but the echoes of their own attack. By their cannoneers this silence is interpreted to mean that the ammunition has given out, and that the Federal position is now assailable. The Confederate fire ceases. Its silence is ominous: it is the calm that just precedes the maddest fury of the storm.

Pickett rides up to Longstreet and asks for orders to advance. The movement is so contrary to Longstreet's judgment, that that general is silent. He answers nothing. Pickett says to his superior, proudly: "I shall go forward, sir!" And then, from out the woods which contain the Confederate fortified line, there bursts a splendid mass of infantry, which is quickly marshaled in magnificent line of battle. It is a compact formation, fourteen thousand strong. At the word, the men start forward:

> Firm-paced and slow, a horrid front they form,
> Still as the breeze, but dreadful as the storm!

Nothing interrupts the view of this superb movement. The dullest soldier can comprehend as readily as his general the purpose and power of this advancing host. The shock will be great—possibly fatal! Full of ardor as if rushing to assault the capital of the nation, yet marching with measured steps so as not to break the alignment, on come these valiant men, treading steadily forward, while yet aware that each step brings them nearer certain death. Solidly quiet, magnificent is their progress. Marching in the direction of the salient position occupied by Hancock, Pickett, after passing beyond the front of Wilcox, causes each of his brigades to make a half-wheel to the left. This movement is hardly completed before McGilvery leads off with the fire of the Federal batteries: a cloud-burst of flame. This, though well directed, does not suffice to check the soldiers of Pickett. Another half-wheel to the right, and Pickett is in a perilous position. Wilcox has separated from him, and uncovered his right; Pettigrew, on his left, either cannot or will not push forward his supports, and the Federal line is within musket-range. Still the advance is unchecked: Pickett cannot go back. Solid shot, shells, shrapnel, and canister are poured forth in unstinted measure.

Never was a grander sight, never a more matchless courage. Carnage is here and now personified. A single shot of McGilvery, firing upon Pickett's flank, kills ten men. Then the Union infantry pours in a volley. Pickett's front rank is decimated in a second. Staggering a moment, it moves again. The men rush forward at double-quick. The furious fusilade is uninterrupted. Garnett, whose brigade is in the advance, falls dead within a hundred yards of the Union front. His men rush madly upon the parts of the line where are the 69th and 71st. This brings them under the fire of Stannard's brigade, which has occupied a small woods in advance and to the left of the point of Pickett's attack. Hancock, always alert to seize a favorable opportunity, forms them to take the enemy's line in flank. Two regiments from Armistead's right are decimated and disorganized by this movement. The remainder of this brigade throws itself in the rear of the center of Pickett's line. Armistead, urging his men forward, reaches the front rank between Kemper and Garnett—if it yet be possible to distinguish regiments and brigades in this compact mass of human beings, which, all covered with blood, seems to be driven by an irresistible force superior to the individual will of those composing it—and throws himself upon the Union line. The shock is terrific: it falls first on the brigades of Hall and Harrow, then concentrates itself on that of Webb. The Confederates pierce the first line of the Federals, but the latter fall back upon the second small earthworks near the artillery. These pieces now fire grape-shot. Hancock and Gibbon hurry up the reserves. Hall rectifies his line, which has been outflanked on the right, Harrow advances with his left, and almost takes Pickett in reverse. The regiments become mixed; commanders do not know where their soldiers are; the fighting is the struggle of a mob. Commands are of no avail: they cannot be heard or obeyed. A clump of trees just within the angle-wall is the Confederate objective point. Armistead, on foot, his hat waving on the point of his sword, rushes forward to attack the battery. With one hundred and fifty devoted men, who will follow him anywhere, he pierces the mass of combatants, passes the earthworks, and reaches Cushing's guns, which can no longer fire for fear of killing friends. Cushing, mortally wounded in both thighs, runs his last serviceable gun down to the fence, and shouts: "Webb, I will give them one more shot." He fires the gun, calls out "Good-by!" and falls dead beside his piece. Armistead answers the challenge: "Give them the cold steel, boys!" and lays his hand upon a gun. But, at that moment, by the side of Cushing, his young and gallant adversary, intrepid Armistead falls, pierced with balls. They both lie at the foot of the clump of trees, which marks the extreme point reached by the Confederates in this, their supremest effort. Where Cushing and Armistead lie is where the tide of invasion stops. The Confederate cause is buried there: there, beneath the blood of as brave soldiers as ever carried sword or faced the march of death. The men who came forward here, when defeated, did not fall back: there was no one left to return.

The brigades of Wilcox and Perry, failing to move with Pickett's division, having sheltered themselves for a moment, no sooner see that Pickett has gone forward and penetrated the Union line, than they hurry up to assault a little further to the south, in Hancock's face. The Union line attacks with vigor, and Stannard attacks the exposed flank from his vantage-ground. But feeble resistance is offered: the assault is over quickly, numbers are taken prisoners, and the grandest charge of the war is spent. The battle of Gettysburg is won. For, with the exception of two spirited and desperate cavalry-contests between Gregg and Hampton, and Kilpatrick and Stuart, the fighting at Gettysburg is finished. Well may the devout follower of the cause of human liberty exclaim, with the commanding general of the Union army: "Thank God!"

THE VALLEY OF THE SHADOW OF DEATH.

What remained of the regiments that crossed the Potomac on their way North, in June, under the command of colonels, recrossed that river in July under the command of corporals. It was thus that proud Army of Northern Virginia returned to the Old Dominion.

The first part of Lee's army to retreat—the wounded—began their weary blood-stained journey on July 4th. General Imboden, who was designated by the Confederate chieftain to undertake the moving of the wounded, was sent for just before midnight, July 3d. An hour later, he saw his chief riding slowly up to headquarters. His horse was walking : its rider was evidently wrapped in profound thought. There were no sentinels on guard save the soft summer moon, which threw sad shadows over the blood-bestrewn field, now and forever lost to this silent man in gray. No staff-officer accompanied him ; he came alone, as if the burden of the day's disaster had stripped him of his friends, as it had of his cause. Riding alone, he seemed the personification of the Lost Cause—lost on the fields of Gettysburg, now covered by thousands of weary men, thousands of wounded, thousands of the dead !

As he approached and noticed the young general, Lee reined up his horse and essayed to dismount. The effort to do so betrayed so much physical exhaustion that Imboden stepped forward to assist him. He alighted, threw his arm across his saddle to rest himself, and, fixing his eyes upon the ground, leaned in silence upon his weary horse, as motionless as a statue. Upon his dignified and expressive features was stamped the deepest seal of sadness. Imboden broke the silence : "General, this has been a hard day on you." Lee looked up and replied mournfully : "Yes, it has been a sad, sad day to us." Then he relapsed into his thoughtful mood again. After a minute, broken only by the strange sounds of night, he straightened up to his full height, and said, with great animation, energy and excitement of manner, in a voice tremulous with emotion : "General, I never saw troops behave more magnificently than Pickett's division of Virginians did to-day in their grand charge upon the enemy. And, if they had been supported as they were to have been—but for some reason not yet fully explained they were not—we would have held the position they so gloriously won at such fearful loss of noble lives, and the day would have been ours."

After a moment he added, almost in a tone of agony: "Too bad! *Too bad!* Oh, too bad!

After a pause, instructions were given, and Imboden started to lead the weary march back to Virginia. Organizing his train, seventeen miles long, he moved at 4 P. M., July 4th. Hardly was he well away from the heavy shadows of Gettysburg when the storm, which had begun at noon, grew to a gale. Canvas was no shield against it, and the poor wounded, lying upon the hard naked boards of the wagon-bodies, were drenched by the pitiless rain. Horses and mules, blinded and maddened by the storm, became almost unmanageable. The roar of the winds and waters made it almost impossible to communicate orders. From the rapidly-moving wagons, now partly covered by the falling night, issued wails of agony. The men were wounded and mutilated in every conceivable way. Some had their legs shattered by a shell or minie-ball, some were shot through their bodies, others had arms torn to shreds, some had received a ball in the face, or a jagged piece of shell had lacerated their heads. Scarcely one in a hundred had received adequate surgical aid. Many had been without food for thirty-six hours. Their ragged, bloody and dirty clothes, clotted and hardened with blood, rasped the tender inflamed lips of their gaping wounds. Very few of the wagons had even straw in them, and all were without springs. The road was rough and rocky; the jolting was enough to have killed strong men. As the horses trotted on, while the winds howled through the driving rain, there arose, from that awful procession of the dying, oaths and curses, sobs and prayers, moans and shrieks, that pierced the darkness and made the storm seem gentle:

"Oh, God! why can't I die?"

"My God! will no one have mercy on me, and kill me, and end my misery?"

"Oh, stop one minute! Take me out; let me die on the roadside."

"I am dying! I am dying! My poor wife—my dear children—what will become of you?"

No help could be rendered to anyone. There was no time even to press a canteen to the lips of the dying. On, on, was the only thing, on into the night and storm—into the Valley of the Shadow of Death—into oblivion. The battle was lost; the cause was decided. Liberty was triumphant; slavery was abolished in the American republic forever.

A word must be said, before leaving the story of the battle, as there will be many queries, about John Burns, who fought in the ranks with the 142d Regiment. Here are the words of Bret Harte which have given Burns immortality. They are not absolutely accurate, but represent the popular sentiment concerning the part which he bore in the great battle:

> Have you heard the story the gossips tell
> Of John Burns, of Gettysburg? No? Ah well,
> Brief is the glory that hero earns,
> Briefer the story of poor John Burns;
> He was the fellow who won renown—
> The only man who didn't back down
> When the rebels rode through his native town;
> But held his own in the fight next day,
> When all his townsfolk ran away.
> That was in July, sixty-three—
> The very day that General Lee,
> The flower of Southern chivalry,
> Baffled and beaten, backward reeled
> From a stubborn Meade and a barren field.
>
> I might tell how, but the day before,
> John Burns stood at his cottage door,
> Looking down the village street;
> Where, in the shade of his peaceful vine,
> He heard the low of his gathered kine,
> And felt their breath with incense sweet;
> Or, I might say, when the sunset burned
> The old farm gable, he thought it turned
> The milk, that fell in a babbling flood,
> Into the milk-pail, red as blood;
> Or how he fancied the hum of bees
> Were bullets buzzing among the trees.
> But all such fanciful thoughts as these
> Were strange to a practical man like Burns,
> Who minded only his own concerns,
> Troubled no more by fancies fine
> Than one of his calm-eyed long-tailed kine—
> Quite old-fashioned and matter-of-fact,
> Slow to argue, but quick to act.

BATTLE OF GETTYSBURG.

That was the reason, as some folks say,
He fought so well on that terrible day.

And it was terrible. On the right
Raged for hours the heavy fight,
Thundered the battery's double-bass—
Difficult music for men to face;
While on the left—where now the graves
Undulate like the living waves
That all the day unceasing swept
Up to the pits the rebels kept—
Round-shot ploughed the upland glades,
Sown with bullets, reaped with blades;
Shattered fences here and there
Tossed their splinters in the air;
The very trees were stripped and bare;
The barns that once held yellow grain
Were heaped with harvests of the slain:
The cattle bellowed on the plain,
The turkeys screamed with might and main,
And brooding barn-fowl left their rest
With strange shells bursting in each nest.
Just where the tide of battle turns,
Erect and lonely, stood old John Burns.

How do you think the man was dressed?
He wore an ancient long buff vest—
Yellow as saffron, but his best;
And buttoned over his manly breast
Was a bright blue coat, with a rolling collar
And large gilt buttons—size of a dollar—
With tails that country-folk call "swaller."
He wore a broad-brimmed bell-crowned hat,
White as the locks on which it sat.
Never had such a sight been seen
For forty years on the village green,
Since John Burns was a country beau,
And went to the "quilting," long ago.

Close at his elbows, all that day,
Veterans of the Peninsula,
Sunburnt and bearded, charged away,

And striplings, downy of lip and chin—
Clerks that the Home Guard mustered in—
Glanced, as they passed, at the hat he wore,
Then at the rifle his right hand bore,
And hailed him, from out their youthful lore,
With scraps of a slangy repertoire:
"How are you, White Hat?" "Put her through!"
"Your head's level!" and "Bully for you?"
Called him "Daddy," and begged he'd disclose
The name of the tailor who made his clothes,
And what was the value he set on those;
While Burns, unmindful of jeer and scoff,
Stood there picking the rebels off—
With his long brown rifle and bell-crown hat,
And the swallow-tails they were laughing at.

'Twas but a moment: for that respect
Which clothes all courage their voices checked;
And something the wildest could understand
Spake in the old man's strong right hand,
And his corded throat, and the lurking frown
Of his eyebrows under his old bell-crown;
Until, as they gazed, there crept an awe
Through the ranks, in whispers, and some men saw,
In the antique vestments and long white hair,
The Past of the Nation in battle there.
And some of the soldiers since declare
That the gleam of his old white hat afar,
Like the crested plume of the brave Navarre,
That day was their oriflamme of war.
Thus raged the battle. You know the rest:
How the rebels, beaten and backward pressed,
Broke at the final charge and ran;
At which John Burns, a practical man,
Shouldered his rifle, unbent his brows,
And then went back to his bees and cows.

This is the story of old John Burns—
This is the moral the reader learns:
In fighting the battle, the question's whether
You'll show a hat that's white, or a feather.

SELECTIONS.

THE following are a few songs, selections and clippings for the entertainment and amusement of those who may wish to read them.

BATTLE HYMN OF THE REPUBLIC.

[November, 1861.]

Mine eyes have seen the glory of the coming of the Lord ;
He is trampling out the vintage where the grapes of wrath are stored ;
He hath loosed the fateful lightning of His terrible swift sword :
    His truth is marching on.

I have seen Him in the watch-fires of a hundred circling camps ;
They have builded Him an altar in the evening dews and damps ;
I have read His righteous sentence by the dim and flaring lamps :
    His day is marching on.

I have read a fiery gospel writ in burnished rows of steel :
" As ye deal with my contemners, so with you my grace shall deal ;
Let the Hero, born of woman, crush the serpent with his heel,
    Since God is marching on."

He has sounded forth the trumpet that shall never call retreat ;
He is sifting out the hearts of men before His judgment-seat ;
Oh, be swift, my soul, to answer Him ! be jubilant, my feet !
    Our God is marching on.

In the beauty of the lilies Christ was born across the sea,
With a glory in His bosom that transfigures you and me ;
As He died to make men holy, let us die to make men free,
    While God is marching on.

THE RED, WHITE AND BLUE.

O Columbia, the gem of the ocean,
    The home of the brave and the free;
The shrine of each patriot's devotion,
    A world offers homage to thee.
Thy mandates make heroes assemble
    When Liberty's form stands in view;
Thy banners make tyranny tremble,
    When borne by the Red, White and Blue.

CHORUS—When borne by the Red, White and Blue,
    When borne by the Red, White and Blue,
    Thy banners make tyranny tremble,
    When borne by the Red, White and Blue.

When war winged its wide desolation,
    And threatened the land to deform,
The ark then of freedom's foundation,
    Columbia rode safe through the storm;
With her garlands of victory around her,
    When so proudly she bore her brave crew;
With her flag proudly floating before her,
    The boast of the Red, White and Blue.

CHORUS—The boast of the Red, White and Blue,
    The boast of the Red, White and Blue,
    With her flag proudly floating before her,
    The boast of the Red, White and Blue.

The wine cup, the wine cup, bring hither
    And fill you it true to the brim;
May the wreaths they have won never wither,
    Nor the star of their glory grow dim.
May the service united never sever,
    But they to their colors prove true,
The Army and Navy forever,
    Three cheers for the Red, White and Blue.

CHORUS—Three cheers for the Red, White and Blue,
    Three cheers for the Red, White and Blue,
    The Army and Navy forever,
    Three cheers for the Red, White and Blue.

BARBARA FRIETCHIE.

[The incidents which gave rise to this poem are said to have occurred during Stonewall Jackson's march through Frederick City, Maryland, just before the battle of South Mountain, in September, 1862. Some of the facts narrated having been called in question, Mr. Whittier furnished the editor of " Bugle Echoes" (November 15, 1885) with the following particulars : "Of the substantial truth of the heroism of Barbara Frietchie I can have no doubt. Mrs. E. D. N. Southworth, the novelist, of Washington, sent me a slip from a newspaper, stating the circumstances as it is given in the poem, and assured me of its substantial correctness. Dorothea L. Dix, the philanthropic worker in the Union hospitals, confirmed it. From half a dozen other sources I had the account, and all agree in the main facts. Barbara Frietchie was the boldest and most outspoken Unionist in Frederick, and manifested it to the Rebel army in an unmistakable manner."]

Up from the meadows rich with corn,
Clear in the cool September morn,

The clustered spires of Frederick stand
Green-walled by the hills of Maryland.

Round about them orchards sweep,
Apple and peach tree fruited deep,

Fair as a garden of the Lord
To the eyes of the famished rebel horde.

On that pleasant morn of the early fall
When Lee marched over the mountain wall—

Over the mountains, winding down,
Horse and foot into Frederick town.

Forty flags with their silver stars,
Forty flags with their crimson bars,

Flapped in the morning wind : the sun
Of noon looked down and saw not one.

Up rose old Barbara Frietchie then,
Bowed with her fourscore years and ten ;

Bravest of all in Frederick town,
She took up the flag the men hauled down ;

In her attic window the staff she set,
To show that one heart was loyal yet.

SELECTIONS.

Up the street came the rebel tread,
Stonewall Jackson riding ahead.

Under his slouched hat left and right
He glanced: the old flag met his sight.

"Halt!"—the dust-brown ranks stood fast;
"Fire!"—out blazed the rifle-blast.

It shivered the window, pane and sash;
It rent the banner with seam and gash.

Quick, as it fell, from the broken staff
Dame Barbara snatched the silken scarf;

She leaned far out on the window-sill,
And shook it forth with a loyal will.

"Shoot, if you must, this old gray head,
But spare your country's flag," she said.

A shade of sadness, a blush of shame,
Over the face of the leader came;

The nobler nature within him stirred
To life at that woman's deed and word:

"Who touches a hair of yon gray head
Dies like a dog! March on!" he said.

All day long through Frederick street
Sounded the tread of marching feet;

All day long that free flag tost
Over the heads of the rebel host.

Ever its torn folds rose and fell
On the loyal winds that loved it well;

And through the hill-gaps sunset light
Shown over it with a warm good-night.

Barbara Frietchie's work is o'er,
And the Rebel rides on his raids no more.

Honor to her! and let a tear
Fall, for her sake, on Stonewall's bier.

Over Barbara Frietchie's grave,
Flag of Freedom and Union, wave!

Peace and order and beauty draw
Round thy symbol of light and law;

And ever the stars above look down
On the stars below in Frederick town!
—*John Greenleaf Whittier.*

MARCHING THROUGH GEORGIA.

Bring the good old bugle, boys, we'll sing another song,
Sing it with a spirit that will start the world along—
Sing it as we used to sing it, fifty thousand strong,
    While we were marching through Georgia.

CHORUS.

Hurrah! hurrah! we bring the jubilee!
Hurrah! hurrah! the flag that makes you free!"
So we sang the chorus from Atlanta to the sea,
    While we were marching through Georgia.

How the darkeys shouted when they heard the joyful sound!
How the turkeys gobbled which our commissary found!
How the sweet potatoes even started from the ground,
    While we were marching through Georgia.—CHO.

Yes, and there were Union men who wept with joyful tears,
When they saw the honor'd flag they had not seen for years!
Hardly could they be restrained from breaking forth in cheers,
    While we were marching through Georgia.—CHO.

"Sherman's dashing Yankee boys will never reach the coast!"
So the saucy rebels said, and 'twas a handsome boast.
Had they not forgot, alas! to reckon with the host,
    While we were marching through Georgia?—CHO.

So we made a thoroughfare for Freedom and her train,
Sixty miles in latitude—three hundred to the main;
Treason fled before us, for resistance was in vain,
    While we were marching through Georgia.—CHO.

SHERIDAN'S RIDE.

[During General Sheridan's temporary absence his troops in the Shenandoah Valley were surprised and routed by the Confederates under General Early. The Union commander hurried to the front in time to rally his forces and turn defeat into victory—October 19, 1864.]

Up from the South at break of day,
Bringing to Winchester fresh dismay,
The affrighted air with a shudder bore,
Like a herald in haste, to the chieftain's door,
The terrible grumble, and rumble, and roar,
Telling the battle was on once more,
And Sheridan twenty miles away.

And wider still those billows of war.
Thundered along the horizon's bar ;
And louder yet into Winchester rolled
The roar of that red sea uncontrolled,
Making the blood of the listener cold,
As he thought of the stake in that fiery fray,
And Sheridan twenty miles away.

But there is a road from Winchester town,
A good broad highway leading down ;
And there, through the flush of the morning light,
A steed as black as the steeds of night
Was seen to pass, as with eagle flight ;
As if he knew the terrible need,
He stretched away with his utmost speed ;
Hills rose and fell ; but his heart was gay,
With Sheridan fifteen miles away.

Still sprung from those swift hoofs, thundering South,
The dust, like smoke from the cannon's mouth,
Or the trail of a comet, sweeping faster and faster,
Foreboding to traitors the doom of disaster.
The heart of the steed and the heart of the master

SELECTIONS.

Were beating like prisoners assaulting their walls,
Impatient to be where the battle-field calls ;
Every nerve of the charger was strained to full play,
With Sheridan only ten miles away.

Under his spurning feet the road
Like an arrowy Alpine river flowed,
And the landscape sped away behind
Like an ocean flying before the wind,
And the steed, like a barque fed with furnace ire,
Swept on, with his wild eye full of fire.
But lo ! he is nearing his heart's desire ;
He is snuffing the smoke of the roaring fray,
With Sheridan only five miles away.

The first that the General saw were the groups
Of stragglers, and then the retreating troops.
What was done ? what to do ?—a glance told him both ;
Then striking his spurs with a terrible oath,
He dashed down the line, 'mid a storm of huzzas,
And the wave of retreat checked its course there, because
The sight of the master compelled it to pause.
With foam and with dust the black charger was gray ;
By the flash of his eye, and his red nostril's play,
He seems to the whole great army to say :
"I have brought you Sheridan all the way
From Winchester down to save the day ! "

Hurrah, hurrah for Sheridan !
Hurrah, hurrah for horse and man !
And when their statues are placed on high,
Under the dome of the Union sky,—
The American soldiers' Temple of Fame,—
There with the glorious General's name
Be it said in letters both bold and bright :
" Here is the steed that saved the day
By carrying Sheridan into the fight,
From Winchester,—twenty miles away ! "

— Thomas Buchanan Read.

SCOTT AND THE VETERAN.

[*May, 1861.*]

An old and crippled veteran to the War Department came;
He sought the Chief who led him on many a field of fame—
The Chief who shouted "Forward!" where'er his banner rose,
And bore its stars in triumph behind the flying foes.

"Have you forgotten, General," the battered soldier cried,
"The days of Eighteen Hundred Twelve, when I was at your side?
Have you forgotten Johnson, that fought at Lundy's Lane?
'Tis true I'm old and pensioned, but I want to fight again."

"Have I forgotten?" said the Chief; "my brave old soldier, no!
And here's the hand I gave you then, and let it tell you so:
But you have done your share, my friend; you're crippled, old, and gray,
And we have need of younger arms and fresher blood to-day."

"But, General," cried the veteran, a flush upon his brow,
"The very men who fought with us, they say, are traitors now;
They've torn the flag of Lundy's Lane—our old red, white and blue;
And while a drop of blood is left, I'll show that drop is true.

"I'm not so weak but I can strike, and I've a good old gun
To get the range of traitors' hearts, and pick them, one by one.
Your Minié rifles, and such arms, it a'n't worth while to try;
I couldn't get the hang o' them, but I'll keep my powder dry!"

"God bless you, comrade!" said the Chief; "God bless your loyal heart!
But younger men are in the field, and claim to have their part;
They'll plant our sacred banner in each rebellious town,
And woe, henceforth, to any hand that dares to pull it down!"

"But, General"—still persisting, the weeping veteran cried,
"I'm young enough to follow, so long as your my guide;
And some, you know, must bite the dust, and that, at least can I,—
So give the young ones place to fight, but me a place to die!

"If they should fire on Pickens, let the colonel in command
Put me upon the rampart, with the flag-staff in my hand:
No odds how hot the cannon-smoke, or how the shells may fly;
I'll hold the Stars and Stripes aloft, and hold them till I die!

" I'm ready, General, so you let a post to me be given,
Where Washington can see me, as he looks from highest heaven,
And say to Putnam at his side, or, may be, General Wayne :
'There stands old Billy Johnson, that fought at Lundy's Lane !'

" And when the fight is hottest, before the traitors fly,
When shell and ball are screeching and bursting in the sky,
If any shot should hit me, and lay me on my face,
My soul would go to Washington's and not to Arnold's place !"

—*Bayard Taylor.*

TENTING ON THE OLD CAMP-GROUND.

We are tenting to-night on the old camp-ground,
   Give us a song to cheer
Our weary hearts, a song of home
   And friends we love most dear.

     CHORUS—Many are the hearts that are weary to-night,
        Wishing for the war to cease,
       Many are the hearts looking for the right,
        To see the dawn of peace.
       Tenting to-night, tenting to-night,
       Tenting on the old camp-ground.

We've been tenting to-night on the old camp-ground,
   Thinking of days gone by,
Of the loved ones at home, that gave us the hand,
   And the tear that said good-by.—CHORUS.

We are tired of war on the old camp-ground,
   Many are dead and gone,
Of the brave and true who left their homes—
   Others been wounded long.—CHORUS.

We've been fighting to-day on the old camp-ground,
   Many are lying near ;
Some are dead, and some are dying,
   Many are in tears.

     CHORUS—Dying to-night, etc.

THE STAR-SPANGLED BANNER.

Oh, say, can you see, by the dawn's early light,
  What so proudly we hail'd at the twilight's last gleaming,
Whose broad stripes and bright stars, thro' the perilous fight,
  O'er the ramparts we watch'd, were so gallantly streaming?
And the rockets' red glare, the bombs bursting in air,
  Gave proof thro' the night that our flag was still there.
Oh, say, does that star-spangled banner yet wave
  O'er the land of the free and the home of the brave?

On the shore dimly seen thro' the mists of the deep,
  Where the foe's haughty host in dread silence reposes,
What is that which the breeze, o'er the towering steep,
  As it fitfully blows, half conceals, half discloses?
Now it catches the gleam of the morning's first beam,
  In full glory reflected, now shines on the stream;
'Tis the star-spangled banner: oh, long may it wave
  O'er the land of the free and the home of the brave.

And where is that band who so vauntingly swore,
  That the havoc of war and the battle's confusion,
A home and a country should leave us no more?
  Their blood has washed out their foul footsteps' pollution.
No refuge could save the hireling and slave
  From the terror of flight or the gloom of the grave:
And the star-spangled banner in triumph doth wave
  O'er the land of the free and the home of the brave.

Oh, thus be it ever when freeman shall stand
  Between their loved homes and wild war's desolation;
Blest with vict'ry and peace, may the heav'n-rescued land
  Praise the pow'r that hath made and preserved us a nation!
Then conquer we must, when our cause it is just,
  And this be our motto: "In God is our trust!"
And the star-spangled banner in triumph shall wave
  O'er the land of the free and the home of the brave.

THE SWORD OF BUNKER HILL.

He lay upon his dying bed;
   His eye was growing dim,
When with a feeble voice he called
   His weeping son to him:
"Weep not, my boy!" the vet'ran said,
   I bow to Heaven's high will—
But quickly from yon antlers bring
   The Sword of Bunker Hill;
But quickly from yon antlers bring
   The Sword of Bunker Hill."

The sword was brought, the soldier's eye
   Lit with a sudden flame;
And as he grasped the ancient blade,
   He murmured Warren's name:
Then said, "My boy, I leave you gold—
   But what is richer still,
I leave you, mark me, mark me now—
   The Sword of Bunker Hill;
I leave you, mark me, mark me now—
   The Sword of Bunker Hill.

"'Twas on that dread, immortal day,
   I dared the Briton's band,
A captain raised this blade on me—
   I tore it from his hand:
And while the glorious battle raged
   It lightened freedom's will—
For, boy, the God of freedom blessed
   The Sword of Bunker Hill;
For, boy, the God of freedom blest
   The Sword of Bunker Hill.

"O, keep the sword!"—his accents broke—
   A smile—and he was dead—
But his wrinkled hand still grasped the blade,
   Upon that dying bed.

The son remains ; the sword remains—
  Its glory growing still—
And twenty millions bless the sire
  And Sword of Bunker Hill ;
And twenty millions bless the sire
  And Sword of Bunker Hill.

THE BATTLE-CRY OF FREEDOM.

(RALLYING SONG.)

Yes, we'll rally round the flag, boys, we'll rally once again,
  Shouting the battle-cry of freedom,
We will rally from the hillside, we'll gather from the plain,
  Shouting the battle-cry of freedom.

  CHORUS—The Union forever, hurrah ! boys, hurrah !
      Down with the traitor, up with the star,
  While we rally round the flag, boys, rally once again,
    Shouting the battle-cry of freedom !

We are springing to the call of our brothers gone before,
  Shouting the battle-cry of freedom,
And we'll fill the vacant ranks with a million freemen more,
  Shouting the battle-cry of freedom.

  CHORUS—The Union forever, etc.

We will welcome to our numbers the loyal, true and brave,
  Shouting the battle-cry of freedom,
And altho' he may be poor he shall never be a slave,
  Shouting the battle-cry of freedom.

  CHORUS—The Union forever, etc.

So we're springing to the call from the East and from the West,
  Shouting the battle-cry of freedom,
And we'll hurl the rebel crew from the land we love the best,
  Shouting the battle-cry of freedom.

  CHORUS—The Union forever, etc.

THE COMMON CHORD.

The Rappahannock's stately tide, aglow with sunset light,
Came sweeping down between the hills that hemmed its gathering
    might ;
From one side rose the Stafford slopes, and on the other shore
The Spottsylvania meadows lay, with oak groves scattered o'er.
Hushed were the sounds of busy day ; the brooding air was hushed,
Save for the rapid-flowing stream that chanted as it rushed.
O'er mead and gently-sloping hills, on either side the stream,
The white tents of the soldiers caught the sun's departing beam—
On Spottsylvania's slopes the Blue, on Stafford's hills the Gray ;
Between them like an unsheathed sword, the glittering river lay.
Hark! suddenly a Union band far down the stream sends forth
The strains of "Hail Columbia," the pæan of the North.
The tents are parted ; silent throngs of soldiers, worn and grim,
Stand forth upon the dusky slopes to hear the martial hymn.
So clear and quiet was the night that to the farthest bound
Of either camp was borne the swell of sweet triumphant sound.
And when the last note died away, from distant post to post
A shout like thunder of the tide rolled through the Federal host.
Then straightway from the other shore there rose an answering strain,
"Bonnie Blue Flag" came floating down the slope and o'er the plain.
And then the Boys in Gray sent back our cheer across the tide—
A mighty shout that rent the air and echoed far and wide.
"Star Spangled Banner," we replied ; they answered, "Boys in Gray,"
While cheer on cheer rolled through the dusk, and faintly died away.
Deeply the gloom had gathered round, and all the stars had come,
When the Union band began to play the notes of "Home, Sweet
    Home."
Slowly and softly breathed the chords, and utter silence fell
Over the valley and the hills—on Blue and Gray as well.
Now swelling, now sinking low, now tremulous, now strong,
The leader's cornet played the air of the beautiful old song ;
And rich and mellow, horn and bass joined in the flowing chords,
So voice-like that they scarcely lacked the charm of spoken words.
Then what a cheer from both the hosts, with faces to the stars !
And tears were shed, and prayers were said, upon the field of Mars.
The Southern band caught up the strain ; and we, who could sing,
    sang.

Oh! what a glorious hymn of home across the river rang.
We thought of loved ones far away, of scenes we'd left behind—
The low-roofed farm-house 'neath the elm that murmured in the wind ;
The children standing by the gate, the dear wife in the door ;
Oh! loud and long the cheer we raised, when silence fell again,
And died away among the hills the dear familiar strain.
Then to our cots of straw we stole, and dreamed the livelong night
Of far-off hamlets in the hills, peace-walled, and still, and white.

—James Buckham.

A WARRIOR BOLD.

In days of old, when Knights were bold,
   And Barons held their sway,
A warrior bold, with spurs of gold,
   Sang merrily his lay,—
"My love is young and fair
My love hath golden hair,
   And eyes of blue, and heart so true,
That none with her compare.
   So what care I, tho' death be nigh,
   I'll live for love, or die."

So this brave Knight, in armor bright,
   Went gaily to the fray.
He fought the fight, but ere the night
   His soul had pass'd away.
The plighted ring he wore
Was crush'd and wet with gore,
   Yet ere he died, he bravely cried,—
"I've kept the vow I swore.
   So what care I, tho' death be nigh,
   I've fought for love, and die."

"YES, I'M GUILTY."

"Yes, I am guilty," the prisoner said,
As he wiped his eyes and bowed his head,
"Guilty of all the crimes you name ;
But this yere lad is not to blame.
'Twas I alone who raised the row,
And, Judge, if yer please, I'll tell yer how.
You see, this boy is pale and slim ;
We calls him saint—his name is Tim—
He's like a preacher in his ways :—
He never drinks, or swears, or plays,
But kinder sighs and weeps all day ;—
'Twould break your heart to hear him pray.
Why, sir, many and many a night,
When grub was scarce and I was tight,
No food, no fire, no light to see,
When home was hell, if hell there be,
I've seen that boy in darkness kneel
And pray such words as cut like steel ;
Which somehow warmed and lit the room,
And sorter chased away the gloom.
Smile if you must, but facts are facts,
And deeds are deeds and acts are acts ;
And though I'm black as sin can be,
His prayers have done a heap for me,
And make me think that God, perhaps,
Sent him on earth to save us chaps.
This man what squealed and pulled us in,
He keeps a place called Fiddlers' Inn,
Where fakes, and snides, and lawless scamps
Connive and plot with thieves and tramps.
Well, Tim and me, we didn't know
Just what to do, or where to go,
And so we stayed with him last night,
And this is how we had the fight :
They wanted Tim to take a drink,
But he refused, as you may think,
And told them how the flowing bowl
Contained the fire that killed the soul.

'Drink! Drink!' they cried, 'this foaming beer;
'Twill make you strong and give you cheer.
Let preachers groan and prate of sin,
But give to us the flowing gin!'
Then Tim knelt down beside his chair,
And offered up this little prayer:
'Help me, dear Lord,' the child began,
As down his cheeks the big tears ran,
'To keep the pledge I gave to you,
And make me strong, and good, and true.
I've done my best to do what's right,
But, Lord, I'm sad and weak to-night.
Father, mother, oh plead for me—
Tell Christ I long with you to be!'
'Get up, you brat, don't pray 'round here,'
The landlord yelled with rage and fear,
Then like a brute he hit the lad,
Which made my blood just b'iling mad.
I guess I must uv hurt his head,
For I struck hard for the man that's dead.
No, he hain't no folks or friends but me:
His dad was killed in sixty-three:
Shot at the front, where bursting shell
And cannon sang their song of hell,
And muskets hissed with fiery breath,
As brave men fell to their tune of death.
I promised his father before he died,
As the life-blood rushed from his wounded side,
I promised him, sir, and it gave him joy,
That I'd protect his darling boy.
I simply did what his father would,
And helped the weak, as all men should.
Yes, I knockd him down and blacked his eye,
And used him rough I'll not deny;
But think of it, Judge, a chap like him
Striking the likes of little Tim.
If I did wrong send me below,
But spare the son of comrade Joe.—
You forgive him; and me? Oh, no!
A fact? God bless you! Come, Tim, let's go."

—*J. M. Munyon.*

OUR TWO OPINIONS.

Us two wuz boys when we fell out—
   Nigh to the age uv my youngest now;
Don't rec'lect what 'twuz about,
   Some small diff'rence, I'll allow.
Lived next neighbors twenty years
   A-hatin' each other, me an' Jim—
He havin' his opinyin uv me
   'Nd I havin' my opinyin uv him!

Grew up together 'nd wouldn't speak,
   Courted sisters, 'nd marr'd 'em, too;
Tended same meetin'-house onct a week,
   A-hatin' each other, through an' through!
But when Abe Linkern asked the West
   F'r soldiers, we answered—me an' Jim—
He havin' his opinyin uv me
   'Nd I havin' my opinyin uv him!

But down in Tennessee one night
   Ther wuz sound uv firin' our way,
And the sergeant allowed ther'd be a fight
   With the Johnnie Rebs some time nex' day;
'Nd as I wuz thinkin' uv Lizzie 'nd home
   Jim stood afore me, long 'nd slim—
He havin' his opinyin uv me
   'Nd I havin' my opinyin uv him!

Seemed like we knew ther wuz goin' to be
   Serious trouble f'r me 'nd him—
Us two shuck hands, did Jim 'nd me,
   But never a word from me or Jim!
He went his way 'nd I went mine,
   'Nd into the battle's roar went we—
He havin' his opinyin uv me
   'Nd I havin' my opinyin uv him!

Jim never came back from the war again,
   But I hain't forgot that last, last night,
When, waitin' f'r orders, us two men
   Made up 'nd shuck hands, afore the fight;

'Nd after all, its soothin' to know
  That here I be 'nd yonder's Jim—
He havin' his opinyin uv me
  'Nd I havin' my opinyin uv him !

AMERICA.

My country ! 'tis of thee,
Sweet land of Liberty,
  Of thee I sing :
Land where my fathers died !
Land of the pilgrims' pride !
From every mountain side
  Let freedom ring !

My native country, thee,
Land of the noble, free,
  Thy name I love ;
I love thy rocks and rills,
Thy woods and templed hills :
My heart with rapture thrills
  Like that above.

Let music swell the breeze,
And ring from all the trees
  Sweet freedom's song :
Let mortal tongues awake ;
Let all that breathe partake ;
Let rocks their silence break
  The sound prolong.

Our fathers' God ! to thee,
Author of liberty,
  To thee we sing :
Long may our land be bright
With freedom's holy light ;
Protect us by thy might,
  Great God, our King !

ODE FOR DECORATION-DAY.

Bring flowers to strew again
With fragrant purple rain
Of lilacs, and of roses white and red,
The dwellings of our dead, our glorious dead !
Let the bells ring a solemn funeral chime,
And wild war-music bring anew the time
   When they who sleep beneath
   Were full of vigorous breath,
And in their lusty manhood sallied forth,
   Holding in strong right hand
   The fortunes of the land,
The pride and power and safety of the North !
It seems but yesterday
The long and proud array—
But yesterday when even the solid rock
Shook as with earthquake shock,—
As North and South, like two huge icebergs, ground
Against each other with convulsive bound,
And the whole world stood still
   To view the mighty war,
   And hear the thundrous roar,
While sheeted lightnings wrapped each plain and hill.

Alas ! how few came back
From battle and from wrack !
Alas ! how many lie
Beneath a Southern sky,
Who never heard the fearful fight was done,
And all they fought for won.
Sweeter, I think, their sleep,
More peaceful and more deep,
Could they but know their wounds were not in vain,
Could they but hear the grand triumphal strain,
And see their homes unmarred by hostile tread.
Ah ! let us trust it is so with our dead—

That they the thrilling joy of triumph feel,
And in that joy disdain the foeman's steel.
We mourn for all, but each doth think of one
    More precious to the heart than aught beside—
Some father, brother, husband, or some son
    Who came not back, or coming, sank and died :
    In him the whole sad list is glorified !
" He fell 'fore Richmond, in the seven long days
    When battle raged from morn till blood-dewed eve,
And lies there," one pale widowed mourner says,
    And knows not most to triumph or to grieve.
"My boy fell at Fair Oaks," another sighs ;
" And mine at Gettysburg ! " his neighbor cries,
    And that great name each sad-eyed listener thrills.
I think of one who vanished when the press
Of battle surged along the Wilderness,
    And mourned the North upon her thousand hills.

O gallant brothers of the generous South,
    Foes for a day and brothers for all time !
I charge you by the memories of our youth,
    By Yorktown's field and Montezuma's clime,
Hold our dead sacred—let them quietly rest
In your unnumbered vales, where God thought best !
Your vines and flowers learned long since to forgive,
And o'er their graves a 'broidered mantle weave ;
Be you as kind as they are, and the word
Shall reach the Northland with each summer bird,
And thoughts as sweet as summer shall awake
Responsive to your kindness, and shall make
Our peace the peace of brothers once again,
And banish utterly the days of pain.

And ye, O Northmen ! be ye not outdone
    In generous thought and deed.
We all do need forgiveness, every one ;
    And they that give shall find it in their need

Spare of your flowers to deck the stranger's grave,
    Who died for a lost cause:
A soul more daring, resolute, and brave
    Ne'er won a world's applause!
(A brave man's hatred pauses at the tomb.)
For him some Southern home was robed in gloom,
Some wife or mother looked with longing eyes
Through the sad days and nights with tears and sighs,—
Hope slowly hardening into gaunt Despair.
Then let your foeman's grave remembrance share;
Pity a higher charm to Valor lends,
And in the realms of Sorrow all are friends.
Yes, bring fresh flowers and strew the soldier's grave,
    Whether he proudly lies
    Beneath our Northern skies,
Or where the Southern palms their branches wave!
Let the bells toll and wild war-music swell,
    And for one day the thought of all the past—
    Of all those memories vast—
Come back and haunt us with its mighty spell!
Bring flowers, then, once again,
And strew with fragrant rain
Of lilacs, and of roses white and red,
The dwellings of our dead.

SPEED AWAY.

Speed away! speed away! on thine errand of light!
There's a young heart awaiting thy coming to-night;
She will fondle thee close, she will ask for the lov'd,
Who pine upon earth since the "Day Star" has roved;
She will ask if we miss her, so long is her stay:
Speed away! speed away! speed away!

And, oh! wilt thou tell her, blest bird on the wing,
That her mother hath ever a sad song to sing;
That she standeth alone, in the still quiet night,
And her fond heart goes forth for the being of light,
Who had slept in her bosom, but who would not stay?
Speed away! speed away! speed away!

Go, bird of the silver wing, fetterless now,
Stoop not thy bright pinions on yon mountain's brow;
But hie thee away, o'er rock, river, and glen,
And find our young "Day Star" ere night close again;
Up! onward! let nothing thy mission delay:
Speed away! speed away! speed away!

THE OLD OAKEN BUCKET.

How dear to this heart are the scenes of my childhood,
   When fond recollection presents them to view!
The orchard, the meadow, the deep tangled wildwood,
   And ev'ry loved spot which my infancy knew,
The wide-spreading pond, and the mill that stood by it,
   The bridge and the rock where the cataract fell;
The cot of my father, the dairy-house nigh it,
   And e'en the rude bucket that hung in the well—
The old oaken bucket, the iron-bound bucket,
The moss-cover'd bucket that hung in the well.

That moss-covered bucket I hailed as a treasure,
   For often at noon, when returned from the field,
I found it the source of an exquisite pleasure,
   The purest and sweetest that nature can yield.
How ardent I seized it, with hands that were glowing,
   And quick to the white-pebbled bottom it fell;
Then soon, with the emblem of truth overflowing,
   And dripping with coolness, it rose from the well—
The old oaken bucket, the iron-bound bucket,
The moss-covered bucket arose from the well.

How sweet from the green, mossy brim to receive it,
   As, poised on the curb, it inclined to my lips!
Not a full-blushing goblet could tempt me to leave it,
   Tho' filled with the nectar that Jupiter sips.
And now, far removed from the loved habitation,
   The tear of regret will intrusively swell,
As fancy reverts to my father's plantation,
   And sighs for the bucket that hung in the well—
The old oaken bucket, the iron-bound bucket,
The moss-covered bucket which hangs in the well.

ANNIE LAURIE.

Maxwelton's braes are bonnie,
   Where early fa's the dew,
And 'twas there that Annie Laurie,
   Gave me her promise true,
   Gave me her promise true,
Which ne'er forgot will be,
   And for bonnie Annie Laurie,
I'd lay me down and dee.

Her brow is like the snawdrift,
   Her throat is like the swan;
Her face it is the fairest
   That e'er the sun shone on,
   That e'er the sun shone on,
And dark-blue is her e'e,
   And for bonnie Annie Laurie,
I'd lay me down and dee.

Like dew on th' gowan lying
   Is th' fa' o' her fairy feet,
And like winds in summer sighing,
   Her voice is low and sweet,
   Her voice is low and sweet,
And she's a' the world to me,
   And for bonnie Annie Laurie,
I'd lay me down and dee.

BANTY TIM;
OR,
TILMON JOY'S REMARKS TO THE WHITE MAN'S COMMITTEE AT SPUNKY POINT, ILLINOIS.

I reckon I get your drift, gents,
You 'low the boy shan't stay.
This is a white man's kentry,
An' you're Dimocrats, you say;
An' whereas, and seein', an' wherefore,
The times bein' all out o' jint,
The nigger has got to mosey
From the limits of Spunky Pint.

Wall! let's reason the thing a minit;
I'm an old-fashioned Dimocrat, too,
But I laid my politics out of the way,
To keep till the war was thro',
An' I kim back here allowin'
To vote as I used to do.
But it gravels me like the devil to train
Along with sich fools as you.

And, dog my cats, if I kin see
In all the light o' day
What you've got to do with the question
If Tim shall go or stay;
An' furder than that I gives notis
That if one on you teches the boy
You may check your trunks for a warmer clime
Than you'll find in Illinois.

Why, blame your hearts, jest hear me:
I remember that ungodly day
When our left struck Vicksburgh Heights,
How ripped, an' torn, an' tattered we lay.
When the rest retreated I stayed behind,
Fur reasons sufficient fur me—
A rib caved in an' a leg on a strike,
As I sprawled on that damned glacee.

Lord! how the hot sun went fur us,
An' boiled, an' blistered, an' burned!
How the rebel bullets whizzed 'round us,
When a cuss in his death grip turned!
Till along towards dusk I seen a thing
I couldn't believe fur a spell,
But that nigger, that Tim, was a crawlin' fur me
Thro' a fire-proof, gilt-edge hell!

The rebels seen him as quick as me,
An' the bullets buzzed like bees,
But he gave a jump an' shouldered me
Tho' a shot brought him once to his knees;
An' he packed me up an' kerried me off,
With a dozen stumbles an' falls,
Till he dropped us both in the Union lines,
His black hide riddled with balls!

So, my gentle gazelles, thar's me answer,
An' here stays Banty Tim;
He trumped Death's ace that day for me,
An' I'm not going back on him.
You may resoloot till the cows come home,
But if one on ye teches the boy,
You will wrastle your hash to-night in hell!
Or my name ain't Tilmon Joy.

IN DE LOUISIANA LOWLANDS.

Way down in Louisiana, not many years ago,
There lived a color'd ge'man, his name was Pompey Snow.
He played upon de banjo, and on de tambourine,
And for rattling ob de bones, he was the greatest eber seen.

    CHORUS.—In de Louisiana lowlands, lowlands, lowlands,
        In de Louisiana lowlands, low.

One night old Pompey started off to play for Cæsardum,
But afore he went he fortified with a good stout glass of rum.
When on de road he thought he saw a darkey, tall and grim,
So Pompey laid de banjo down to break de darkey's shin.

    CHO.—In de Louisiana lowlands, etc.

Says he, "Old chap, just move along, or else I'll spoil your face."
But dis darkey didn't seem to move from out his hiding-place.
So drawing back, he crooked his head and drove at him cachunk.
But Pompey made a sad mistake, for 'twas nothing but a stump.

    CHO.—In de Louisiana lowlands, etc.

De stump it proved a little hard, too hard for Pompey's wool,
For when he struck, de hickory knot went through the darkey's skull.
Dey found his banjo by his side, and Pompey lying dead—

    SPOKEN: And, ladies and gentlemen, dis is de first time upon record dat it was ever known of a darkey's ever coming to his death— By de breaking of his head.

    CHO.—In de Louisiana lowlands, etc.

KINGDOM COMING.

Say, darkeys, hab you seen de massa,
  Wid de muffstash on his face,
Go long de road some time dis mornin',
  Like he gwine to leab de place?
He seen a smoke, way up de ribber,
  Whar de Linkum gumboats lay;
He took his hat, an' lef berry sudden,
  An' I spec he's run away!

CHORUS—De massa run—ha, ha!
  De darkey stay—ho, ho!
  It mus' be now de kingdom comin',
  An' de year ob jubilo!

He six foot one way, two foot tudder,
  An' he weigh tree hundred pound,
His coat so big, he couldn't pay de tailor,
  An' it won't go half way round.
He drill so much dey call him cap'an,
  An' he get so drefful tann'd,
I spec he try an' fool dem Yankees
  For to tink he's contraband.

De darkeys feel so lonesome libing
  In de log-house on the lawn,
Dey move dar tings to massa's parlor,
  For to keep it while he's gone.
Dar's wine an' cider in de kitchen,
  An' de darkeys dey'll hab some:
I spose dey'll all be cornfiscated
  When de Linkum sojers come.

De oberseer he make us trouble,
  An' he dribe us round a spell;
We lock him up in de smoke-house cellar,
  Wid de key trown in de well.
De whip is lost, de han'cuff broken,
  But de massa 'll hab his pay;
He's ole enough, big enough, ought to know better
  Dan to went an' run away.

OLD FOLKS AT HOME.

Way down on the Swanee ribber,
    Far, far away,
Dere's whar my heart is turning ebber,
    Dere's whar de old folks stay.
And up and down the whole creation,
    Sadly I roam ;
Still longing for de old plantation,
    And for de old folks at home.

    All de world am sad and dreary,
        Ebry where I roam ;
    Oh ! darkeys, how my heart grows weary,
        Far from de old folks at home.

All round de little farm I wandered,
    When I was young ;
Den many happy days I squandered,
    Many de songs I sung.
When I was playing with my brudder,
    Happy was I ;
Oh ! take me to my kind old mudder,
    Dere let me live and die.

    All de world am sad and dreary, etc.

One little hut among de bushes,
    One dat I love,
Still sadly to my memory rushes,
    No matter where I rove.
When will I see de bees a humming,
    All round de comb ?
When will I hear de banjo tumming,
    Down in my good old home ?

    All de world am sad and dreary, etc.

HOME, SWEET HOME.

'Mid pleasures and palaces though we may roam,
Be it ever so humble, there's no place like home;
A charm from the skies seems to hallow us there,
Which, seek thro' the world, is ne'er met with elsewhere.

    Home, home, sweet, sweet home,
    There's no place like home,
    Oh, there's no place like home.

I gaze on the moon as I tread the drear wild,
And feel that my mother now thinks of her child;
As she looks on that moon from our own cottage door,
Thro' the woodbine whose fragrance shall cheer me no more.

    Home, home, sweet, sweet home,
    There's no place like home,
    Oh, there's no place like home.

An exile from home, splendor dazzles in vain;
Oh, give me my lowly thatched cottage again;
The birds singing gaily, that came at my call;
Give me them, and that peace of mind, dearer than all.

    Home, home, sweet, sweet home,
    There's no place like home,
    Oh, there's no place like home.

WHAT ARE THE WILD WAVES SAYING?

What are the wild waves saying, sister, the whole day long,
That ever, amid our playing, I hear but their low, lone song?
Not by the sea-side only, there it sounds wild and free;
But at night, when 'tis dark and lonely, in dreams it is still with me.
Brother! I hear no singing! 'tis but the rolling waves,
Ever its lone course winging over some ocean cave!
'Tis but the noise of water, dashing against the shore,
And the wind from some bleaker quarter mingling with its roar.
No! no, it is something greater that speaks to the heart alone,
The voice of the great Creator dwells in that mighty tone!

Yes! but the waves seem ever singing the same sad thing;
And vain is my weak endeavor to guess what the surges sing!
What is that voice repeating, ever by night and day?
Is it a friendly greeting, or a warning that calls away?
Brother! the inland mountain, hath it not voice and sound?
Speaks not the dripping fountain, as it bedews the ground?
E'en by the household ingle, curtain'd and clos'd and warm,
Do not our voices mingle with those of the distant storm?
Yes! but there is something greater that speaks to the heart alone,
The voice of the great Creator dwells in that mighty tone!

THE JINERS.

She was about forty-five years old, well dressed, had black hair, rather thin and tinged with gray, and eyes in which gleamed the fires of a determination not easily balked. She walked into the Mayor's office and requested a private interview, and having obtained it, and satisfied herself that the law students were not listening at the keyhole, said slowly, solemnly, and impressively:

"I want a divorce."

"What for? I supposed you had one of the best of husbands," said the Mayor.

"I s'pose that's what everybody thinks; but if they knew what I've suffered in ten years, they'd wonder I hadn't scalded him long ago. I ought to, but for the sake of the young ones I've borne it and said nothing. I've told him, though, what he might depend on, and now the time's come; I won't stand it, young ones or no young ones. I'll have a divorce, and if the neighbors want to blab themselves hoarse about it they can, for I won't stand it another day."

"But what's the matter? Don't your husband provide for you? Don't he treat you kindly?" pursued the Mayor.

"We get victuals enough, and I don't know but he's as true and kind as men in general, and he's never knocked any of us down. I wish he had; then I'd get him into jail, and know where he was of nights," retorted the woman.

"Then what is your complaint against him?"

"Well, if you must know, he's one of them plaguey jiners."

"A what?"

"A jiner—one of them pesky fools that's always jining something. There can't nothing come along that's dark and sly and hidden but he jines it. If anybody should get up a society to burn his house down, he'd jine it just as soon as he could get in; and if he had to pay for it he'd go all the suddener. We hadn't been married more'n two months before he jined the Know Nothin's. We lived on a farm then, and every Saturday night he'd come tearing in before supper, grab a fistful of nut cakes, and go off gnawing them, and that's the last I'd see of him till morning. And every other night he'd roll and tumble in his bed, and holler in his sleep, 'Put none but Americans on guard—George Washington;' and rainy days he would go out in the corn-barn and jab at a picture of King George with an old bagnet that was there. I ought to put my foot down then, but he fooled me so with his lies that I let him go and encouraged him in it.

"Then he jined the Masons. P'raps you know what them be, but I don't, 'cept they think they are of the same kind of critters that built Solomon's temple; and of all the nonsense and gab about worshipful master and square and compasses and sich like that we had in the house for the next six months, you never see the beat. And he's never outgrowed it nuther. What do you think of man, squire, that'll dress himself in a white apron, about big enough for a monkey's bib, and go marching up and down and making motions and talking foolish lingo at a picture of George Washington in a green jacket and an apron covered over with eyes and columns and other queer pictures? Ain't he a loonytick? Well, that's my Sam, and I've stood it as long as I'm goin' to.

"The next lunge the old fool made was into the Odd Fellows. I made it warm for him when he came home and told me he'd jined them, but he kinder pacified me by telling me they are a sort of branch show that took in women, and he'd get me in as soon as he found how to do it. Well, one night he come home and said I'd been proposed, and somebody had blackballed me. Did it himself, of course. Didn't want me around knowing about his goings on. Of course he didn't, and I told him so.

"Then he jined the Sons of Malter. Didn't say nothing to me about it, but sneaked off one night, pretendin' he'd got to sit up with a sick Odd Fellow, and I never found it out, only he come home lookin' like a man who had been through a threshing machine, and I wouldn't do a thing for him until he owned up. And so its gone from bad to wus, jinin' this and that and t'other, till he's worship minister of the Masons, and goodness of hope of the Odd Fellows, and sword swallower of the Finnegan's, and virgin cerus of the Grange, and grand Mogul of the Sons of Indolence, and two-edged tomahawk of the United Order of Red Men, and tale bearer of the Merciful Manikins, and skipper of the Guild Caratrine Columbus, and grand Oriental Bouncer of the Royal Arcaners, and big wizard of the Arabian Nights, and pledge passer of the Reform club, and chief bulger of the Irish Mechanics, and purse keeper of the Order of Canadian Conscience, and double-barrelled dictator of the Knights of the Brass Circles, and standard bearer of the Royal Archangels, and sublime porte of the Onion League, and chief butler of the Celestial Cherubs, and puissant potentate of the Petrified Pollywogs, and goodness only knows what else. I've borne it and borne it, hopin' he'd get 'em all jined after awhile, but 'tain't no use, and when he'd got into a new one, and been made grand guide of the Knights of Horror, I told him I'd quit and I will."

Here the Mayor interrupted, saying :

"Well, your husband is pretty well initiated, that's a fact ; but the court will hardly call that a good cause for divorce. The most of the societies you mention are composed of honorable men with excellent reputations. Many of them, though called lodges, are relief associations and mutual insurance companies, which, if your husband should die, would take care of you and would not see you suffer if you were sick."

"See me suffer when I'm sick ! Take care of me when he's dead ! Well, I guess not ; I can take care of myself when he's dead, and if I can't I can get another ! There's plenty of em ! And they needn't bother themselves when I am sick either. If I want to be sick and suffer, it's none of their business, especially after all the suffering I've had when I ain't sick, because of their carryin's on. And you needn't try to make me believe it's all right, either. I know what it is to live with a man that jines so many lodges that he don't never lodge at home."

"Oh, that's harmless amusement," quietly remarked the Mayor, "and if all that you say about your husband is really as you affirm, it affords strong proof that he must be a man endowed with an unusual amount of earnestness of purpose, as well as a large degree of popularity."

She looked him square in the eyes and said : "I believe you are a jiner yourself."

He admitted that he was to a certain extent, and she arose and said : "I would not have thought it. A man like you, chairman of a Sabbath school,—it's enough to make a woman take pisen ! But

I don't want anything of you. I want a lawyer that don't belong to nobody or nothin'." And she bolted out of the office to hunt up a man that wasn't a jiner.

AULD LANG SYNE.

Should auld acquaintance be forgot,
  And never brought to mind?
Should auld acquaintance be forgot,
  And days of auld lang syne?
For auld lang syne, my dear,
  For auld lang syne;
We'll tak' a cup o' kindness yet
  For auld lang syne.

We twa ha'e run aboot the braes,
  And pu'd the gowans fine;
But we've wander'd mony a weary foot
  Sin' auld lang syne.
For auld lang syne, my dear,
  For auld lang syne;
We'll tak' a cup o' kindness yet
  For auld lang syne.

We twa ha'e sported i' the burn
  Frae mornin' sun till dine,
But seas between us braid ha'e roared
  Sin' auld lang syne.
For auld lang syne, my dear,
  For auld lang syne;
We'll tak' a cup o' kindness yet
  For auld lang syne.

And here's a hand, my trusty frien',
  And gie's a hand o' thine;
We'll tak' a cup o' kindness yet
  For auld lang syne.
For auld lang syne, my dear,
  For auld lang syne;
We'll tak' a cup o' kindness yet
  For auld lang syne.

www.ingramcontent.com/pod-product-compliance
Lightning Source LLC
Chambersburg PA
CBHW030336170426
43202CB00010B/1147